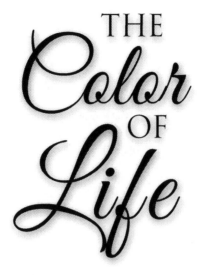

THE Color OF Life

THE LIGHT IN THE DARKNESS

By

LANCE PITTS

TRUTH... that sets you Free

BALBOA
PRESS
A DIVISION OF HAY HOUSE

Balboa Press books may be ordered through booksellers or by contacting:

Balboa Press
A Division of Hay House
1663 Liberty Drive
Bloomington, IN 47403
www.balboapress.com
1 (877) 407-4847

Print information available on the last page.

ISBN: 978-1-5043-6177-4 (sc)
ISBN: 978-1-5043-6178-1 (e)

Balboa Press rev. date: 08/25/2016

CONTENTS

DEDICATION

I dedicate this book to my two sons
Jayden A Pitts, and Ethan E Pitts
As I faced some of the darkest times in my life
The life lessons that taught me
The Truths in this book
You two were the ones that brought me
Back to the path to Life!
You were my Light in the darkness
I'm very grateful for you both!

Thank You!

I LOVE YOU
More than words can express!

Jayden Pitts..
Our first run together.
A Six mile run

Ethan Pitts..
Our first meditation together.
A thirteen minute meditation

A SPECIAL THANK YOU

To the people
That have been part of my Life
You being who you are
Helped me wake up in this Life
And Remember who I AM
I am thankful for my Life
And I will forever
Be Grateful you were in it
May you find the Peace you helped me find!

INTRODUCTION

In 2006 I heard the words REMEMBER ME, in a quiet thought that ran through the back of my Mind. I thought it was God speaking to me, because I had just walked away from my faith, and decided to join the military. At that time, I was going through boot camp, just a few weeks into my training, to become an Infantryman in the United States Army, so I thought God was speaking to me to warn me that military life would put my life in danger because I had walked away from my faith. It would take three years of service in the military before I would figure out that this wasn't the case, but it would take ten years for me to find the understanding of the words REMEMBER ME.

In honor of these words coming to me I now give them to you! May you find their understanding!

Remember Me

I had a Dream
And in this Dream
I could see the Colors of Life
Swimming through the Darkness
As I began to watch the Colors
Move through the Darkness
In that very moment
I understood Life
And Love!

I REMEMBER!

The Body speaks the Word that Creates Life!

Let your Body Speak the Truth!

You find your ability to Create Life
When you express the truth
Of the energies you take in your body
And by following these energies
So that they create
What it is you are here in this life
To Create

YOU!

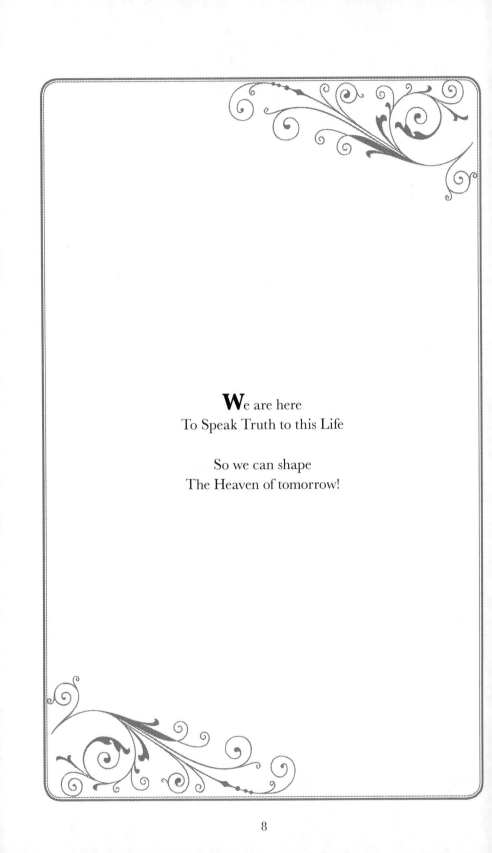

We are here
To Speak Truth to this Life

So we can shape
The Heaven of tomorrow!

But first we have to come back to ourselves!

We have to REMEMBER WHO WE ARE!

We have to come back to Life!

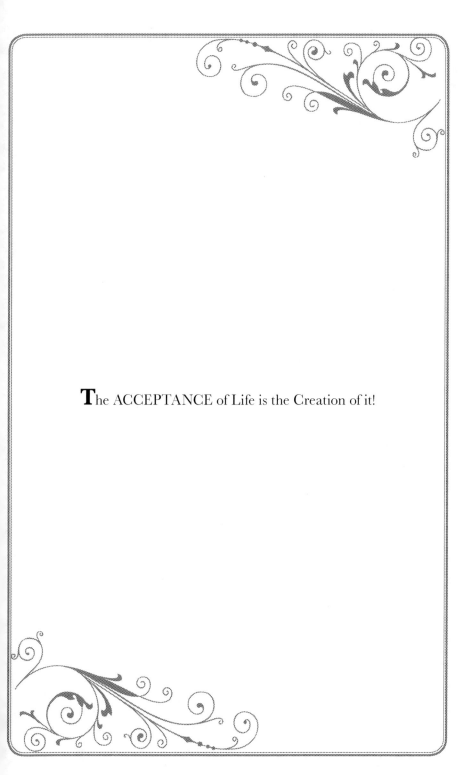

The ACCEPTANCE of Life is the Creation of it!

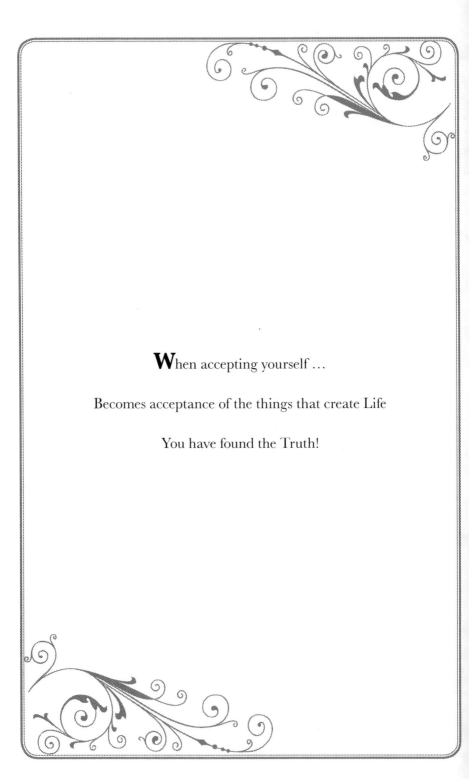

When accepting yourself …

Becomes acceptance of the things that create Life

You have found the Truth!

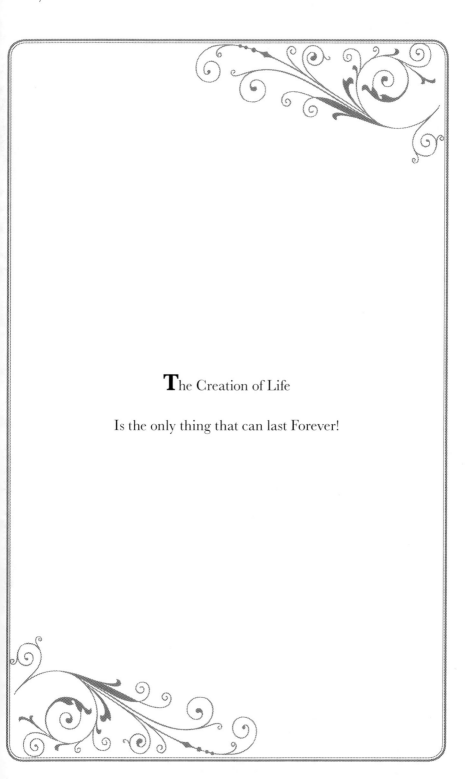

The Creation of Life

Is the only thing that can last Forever!

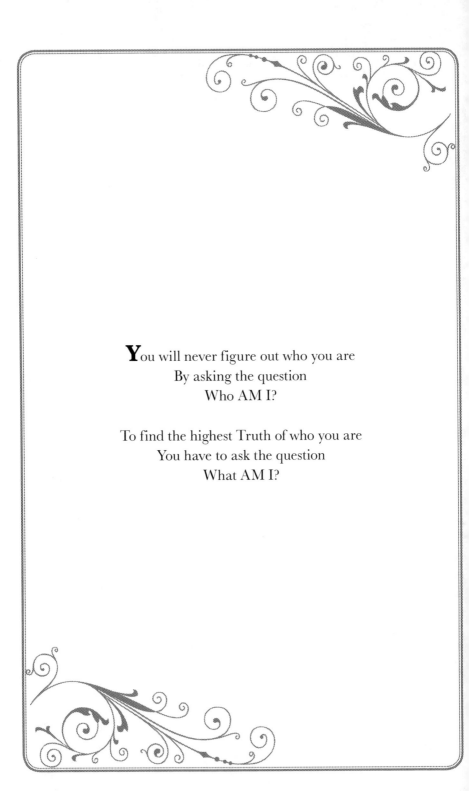

You will never figure out who you are
By asking the question
Who AM I?

To find the highest Truth of who you are
You have to ask the question
What AM I?

You Find yourself when you Remember *What* you are!

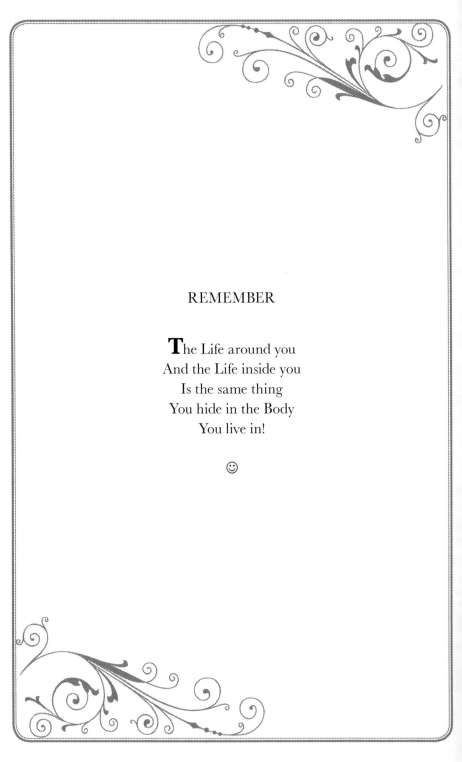

REMEMBER

The Life around you
And the Life inside you
Is the same thing
You hide in the Body
You live in!

☺

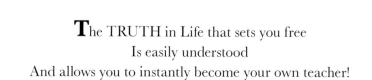

The TRUTH in Life that sets you free
Is easily understood
And allows you to instantly become your own teacher!

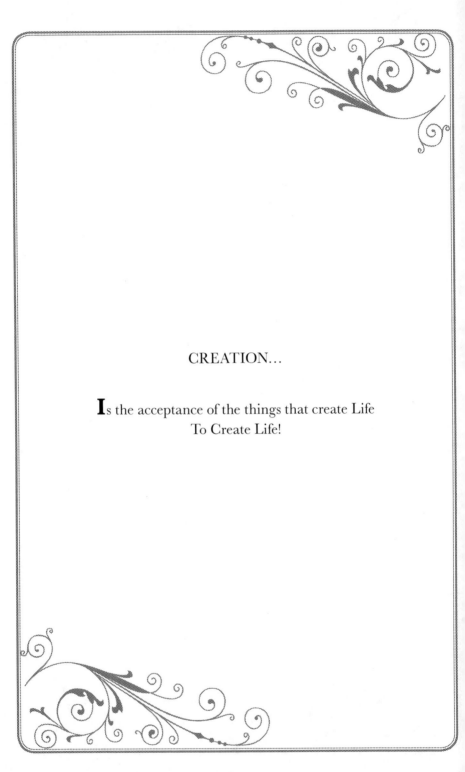

CREATION...

Is the acceptance of the things that create Life
To Create Life!

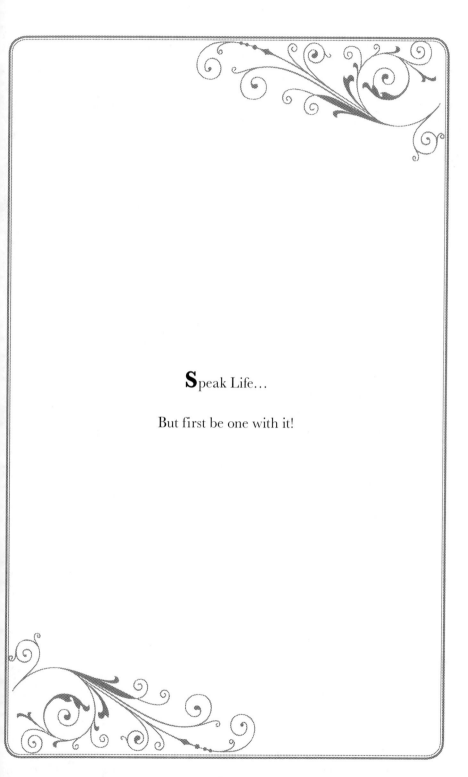

Speak Life…

But first be one with it!

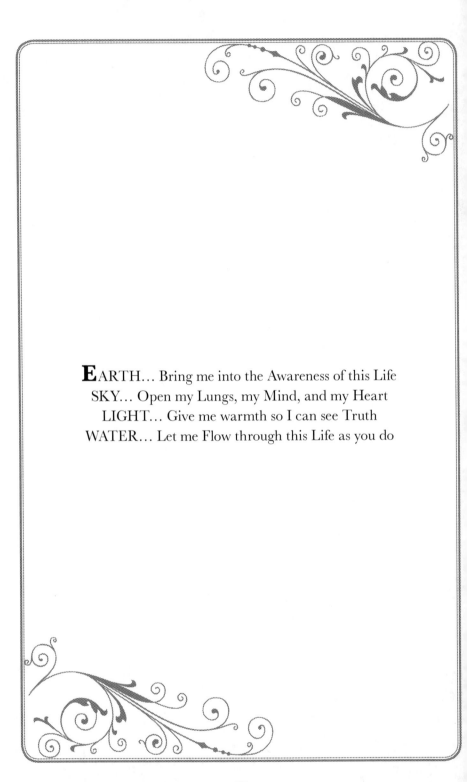

EARTH… Bring me into the Awareness of this Life
SKY… Open my Lungs, my Mind, and my Heart
LIGHT… Give me warmth so I can see Truth
WATER… Let me Flow through this Life as you do

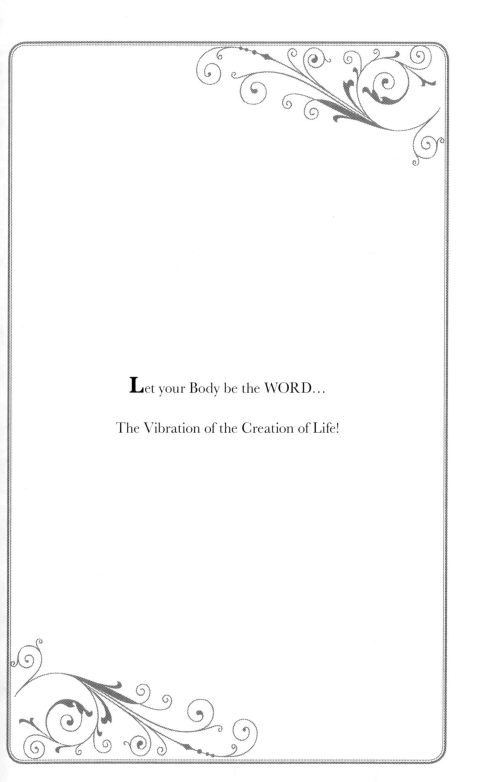

Let your Body be the WORD...

The Vibration of the Creation of Life!

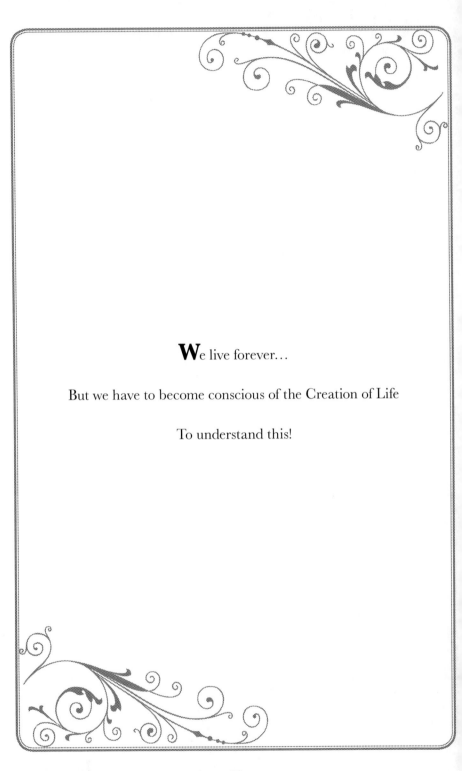

We live forever…

But we have to become conscious of the Creation of Life

To understand this!

The Creator
The Creation of Life
Is so Brilliant
That the only way
To accept it
Is to accept yourself…
LIFE

See how simple the truth is?

LIFE

Is the Truth that sets you Free!!

This is the question that leads us to our Truth
This is the question that reveals to us who we are
This is the question that allows us to remember
How to again find our Peace
With this question we will remove all beliefs about Life
That separate us from our happiness
And be able to see through our many confusions
This question will teach us how to again have Faith in ourselves
And Faith in this Life

WHAT ARE WE?

Separate yourself from all man made creation
And all thought created by man…

WHATS LEFT?

My beliefs and understanding can be summed up in two words

I AM!

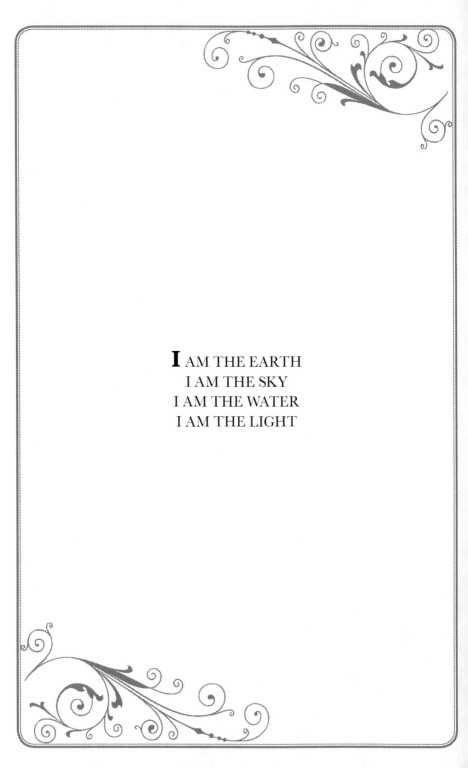

I AM THE EARTH
I AM THE SKY
I AM THE WATER
I AM THE LIGHT

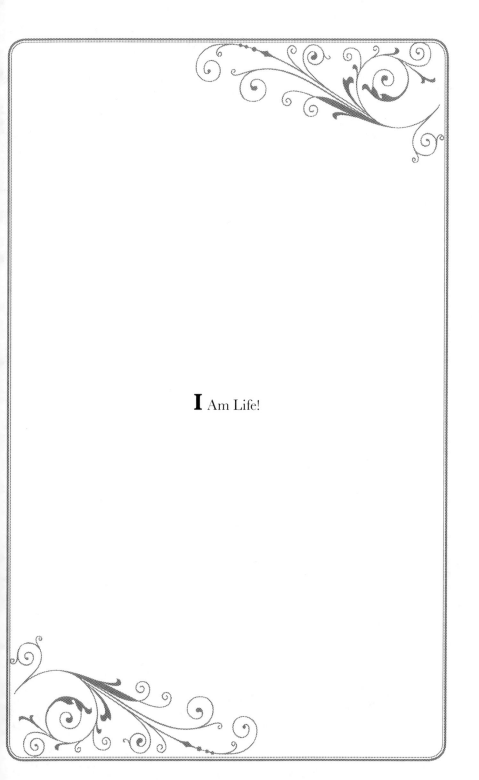

I Am Life!

I AM YOU!

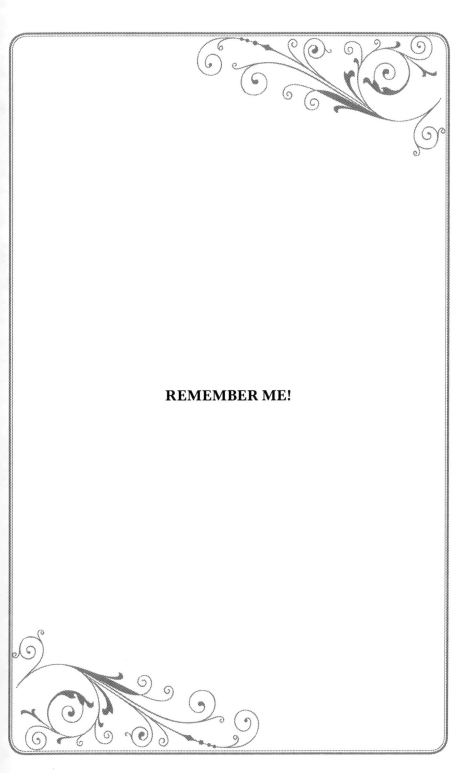

REMEMBER ME!

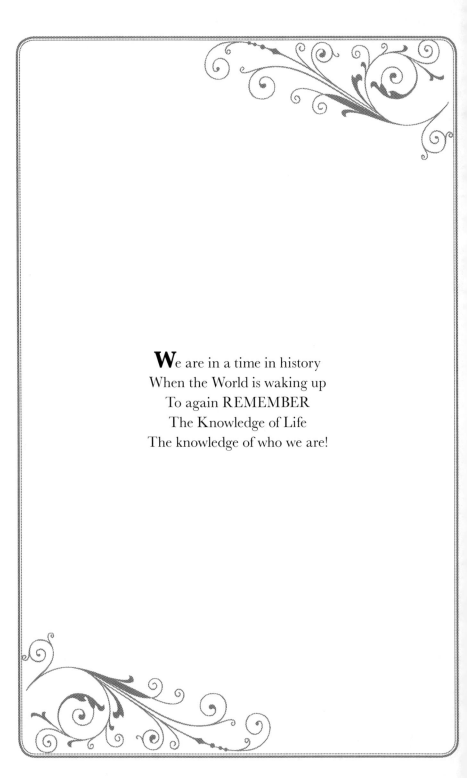

We are in a time in history
When the World is waking up
To again REMEMBER
The Knowledge of Life
The knowledge of who we are!

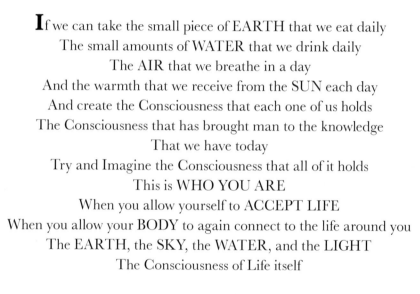

If we can take the small piece of EARTH that we eat daily
The small amounts of WATER that we drink daily
The AIR that we breathe in a day
And the warmth that we receive from the SUN each day
And create the Consciousness that each one of us holds
The Consciousness that has brought man to the knowledge
That we have today
Try and Imagine the Consciousness that all of it holds
This is WHO YOU ARE
When you allow yourself to ACCEPT LIFE
When you allow your BODY to again connect to the life around you
The EARTH, the SKY, the WATER, and the LIGHT
The Consciousness of Life itself

THE BODY

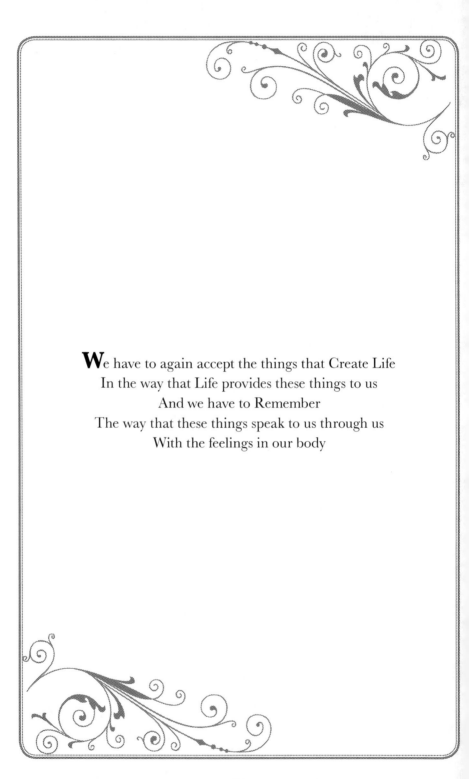

We have to again accept the things that Create Life
In the way that Life provides these things to us
And we have to Remember
The way that these things speak to us through us
With the feelings in our body

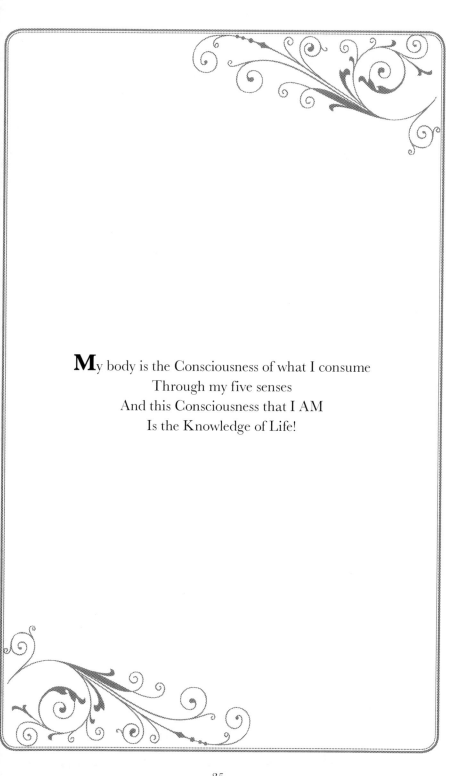

My body is the Consciousness of what I consume
Through my five senses
And this Consciousness that I AM
Is the Knowledge of Life!

I AM

The consciousness of Life itself!

Say this aloud…

I AM Truth!

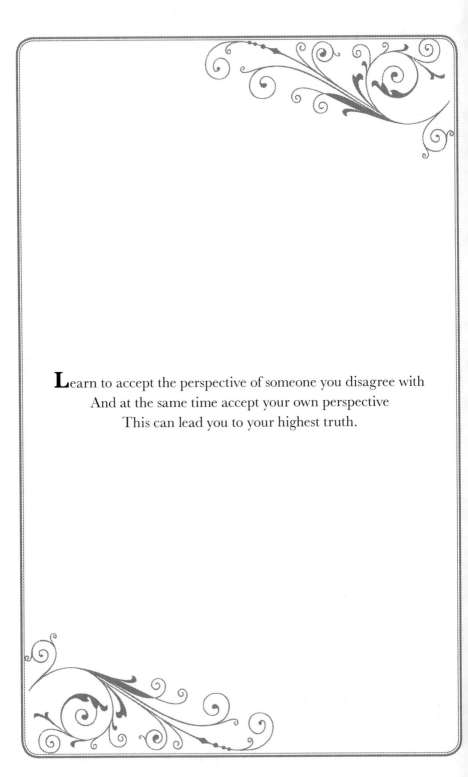

Learn to accept the perspective of someone you disagree with
And at the same time accept your own perspective
This can lead you to your highest truth.

All People speak the truth of their combined life experiences.

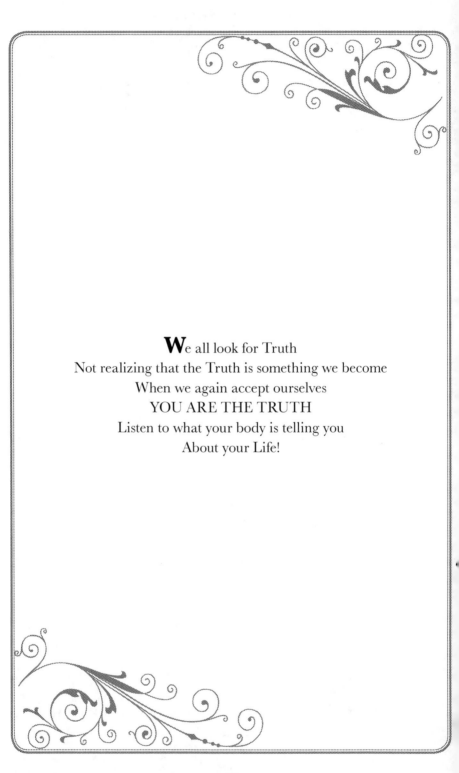

We all look for Truth
Not realizing that the Truth is something we become
When we again accept ourselves
YOU ARE THE TRUTH
Listen to what your body is telling you
About your Life!

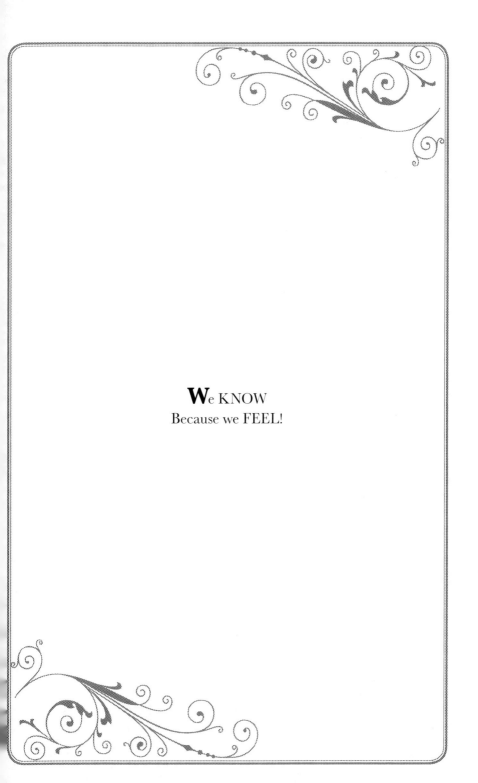

We KNOW
Because we FEEL!

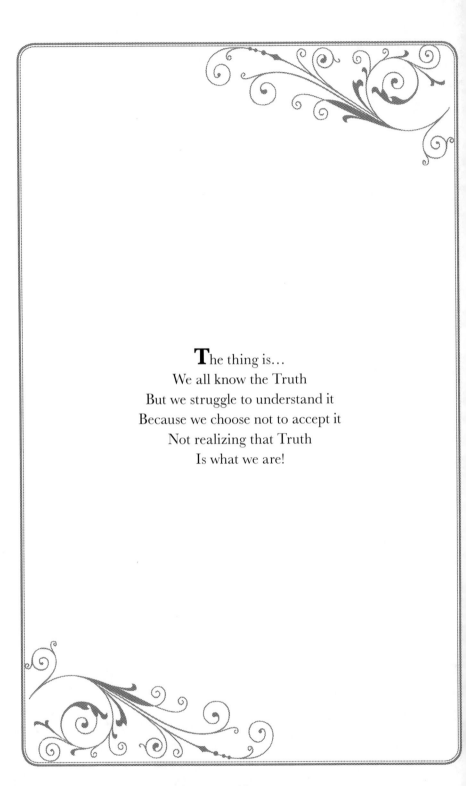

The thing is…
We all know the Truth
But we struggle to understand it
Because we choose not to accept it
Not realizing that Truth
Is what we are!

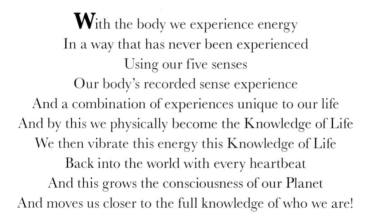

With the body we experience energy
In a way that has never been experienced
Using our five senses
Our body's recorded sense experience
And a combination of experiences unique to our life
And by this we physically become the Knowledge of Life
We then vibrate this energy this Knowledge of Life
Back into the world with every heartbeat
And this grows the consciousness of our Planet
And moves us closer to the full knowledge of who we are!

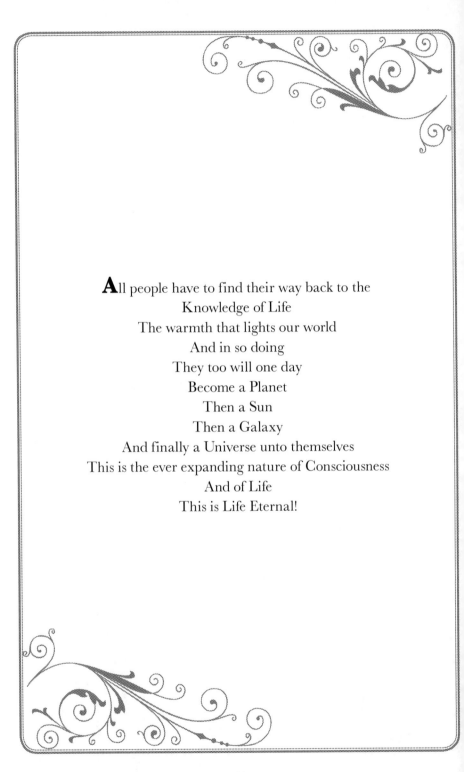

All people have to find their way back to the
Knowledge of Life
The warmth that lights our world
And in so doing
They too will one day
Become a Planet
Then a Sun
Then a Galaxy
And finally a Universe unto themselves
This is the ever expanding nature of Consciousness
And of Life
This is Life Eternal!

Remember me says Life
I am you whispers the Heart

Mankind will one day soon embrace the purpose of Life
And learn that in Health
The Human body is designed to create Light
And as we accept this
In the way that we live
Humanity will finally be able to embrace its purpose
And we will then assist the Stars of Heaven
In Lighting up the Darkness
Of the void from which we come!

What if…

You are the Darkness that allows the Light to shine
And the Light that shines in the night Sky

Grow to be…

Through the evolution of human Consciousness
The Darkness becoming the Light!

In letting our Hearts again create Light
We will help another Planet become a Star!

The thing your Heart desires
Is the ability to Create Life!

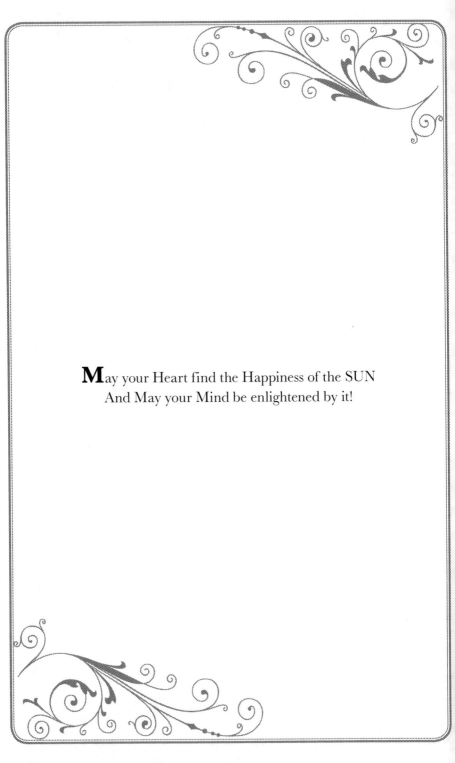

May your Heart find the Happiness of the SUN
And May your Mind be enlightened by it!

Can you see the connection
Between Your body's ability to Create Heat
The Warmth of the Sun and your ability to see?
And can you see why the warmth of Emotion
Is how you see the Higher Truth in life?
And can you see why you need the Light
To Be… and to See The Creation of Life?

I see Humanity assisting the Stars of Heaven
Light up the darkness of the void from which we come
To evolve our consciousness
In the Knowledge of Light
The Knowledge of Love
Opening our Minds to understand
The Knowledge of Life
So that we grow to the Light of a Pure Consciousness
Which is the full Knowledge of who we are!

SELF LOVE

 A movement for change… for a brighter future
It's time to shine our Light!

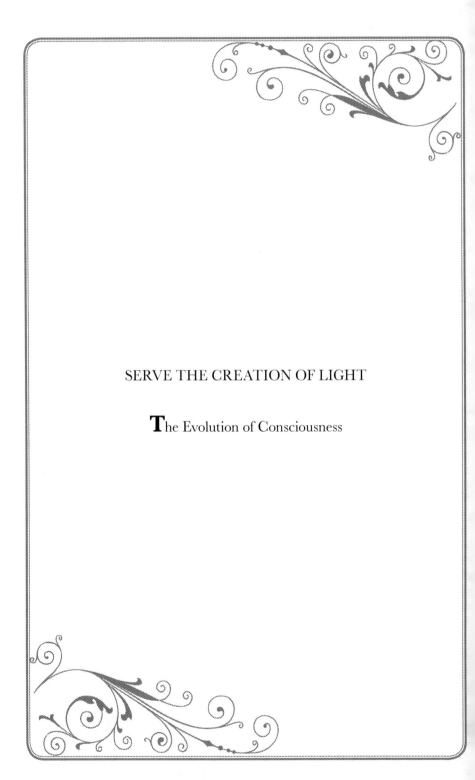

SERVE THE CREATION OF LIGHT

The Evolution of Consciousness

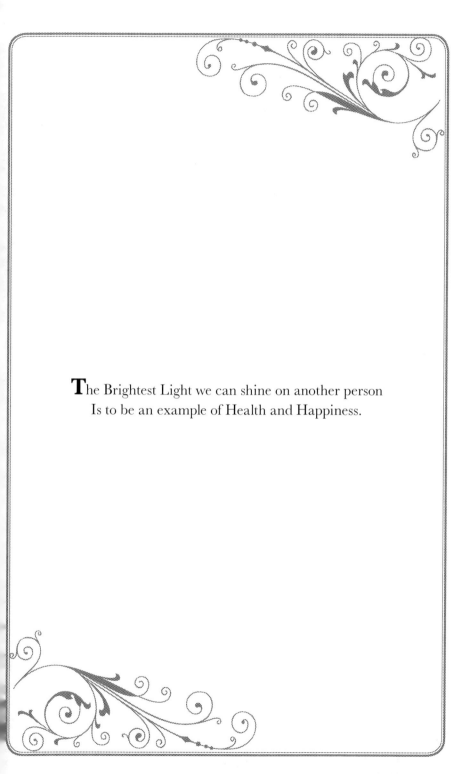

The Brightest Light we can shine on another person
Is to be an example of Health and Happiness.

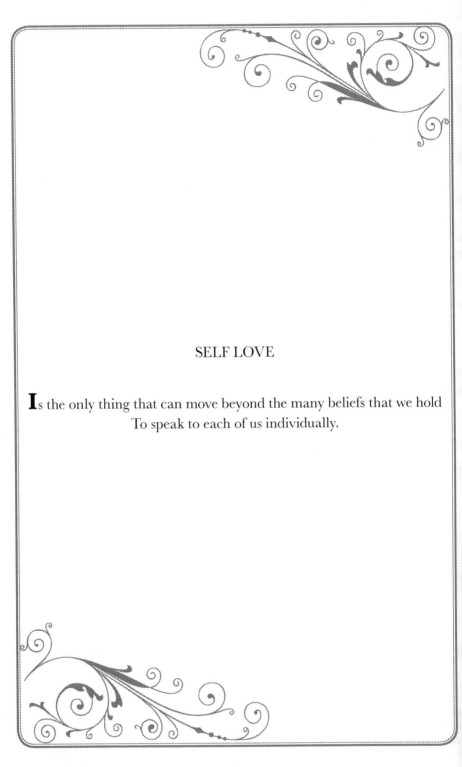

SELF LOVE

Is the only thing that can move beyond the many beliefs that we hold
To speak to each of us individually.

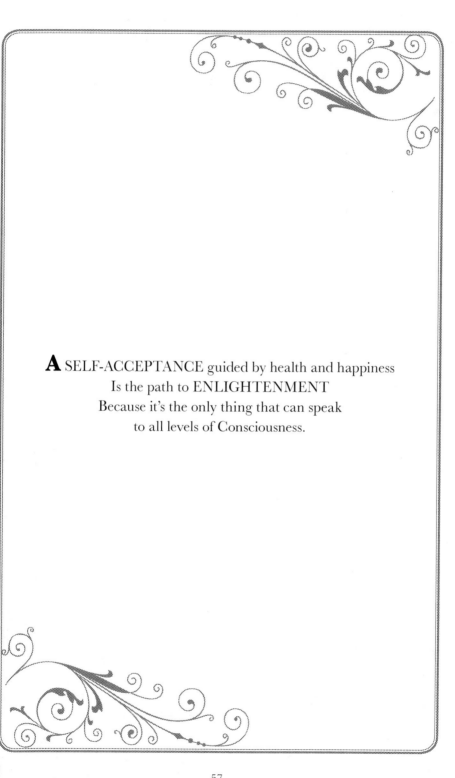

A SELF-ACCEPTANCE guided by health and happiness
Is the path to ENLIGHTENMENT
Because it's the only thing that can speak
to all levels of Consciousness.

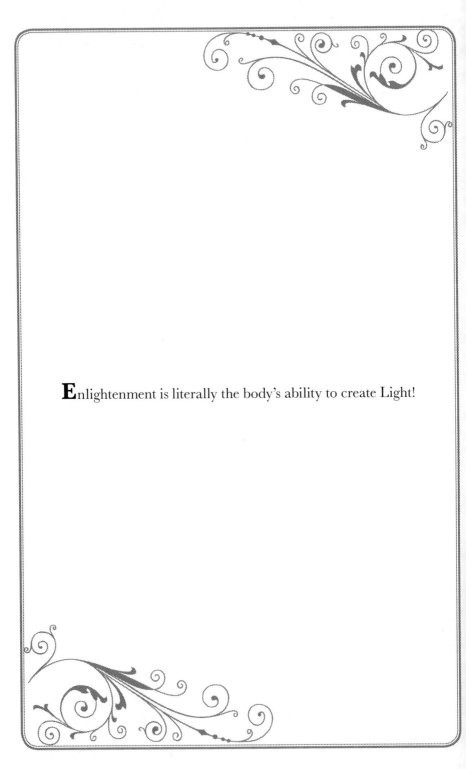

Enlightenment is literally the body's ability to create Light!

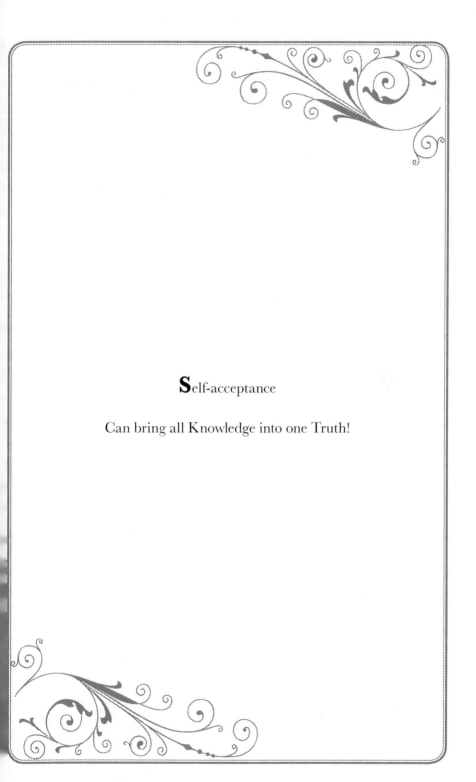

Self-acceptance

Can bring all Knowledge into one Truth!

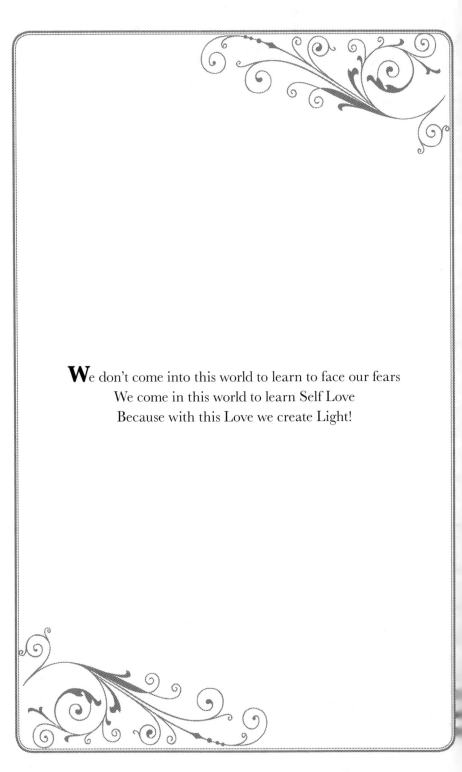

We don't come into this world to learn to face our fears
We come in this world to learn Self Love
Because with this Love we create Light!

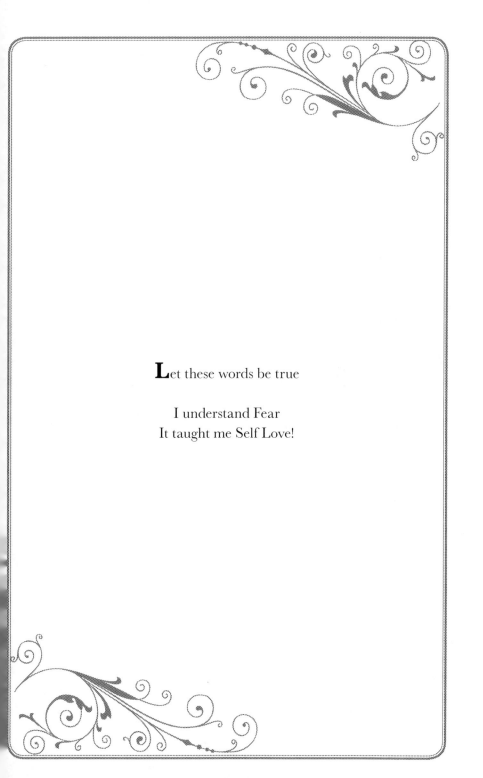

Let these words be true

I understand Fear
It taught me Self Love!

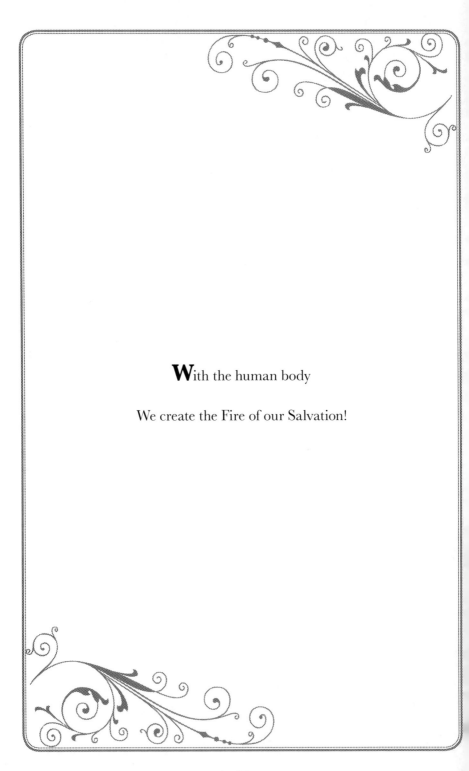

With the human body

We create the Fire of our Salvation!

Consciousness is Light!

As you ascend in consciousness
In your ability to understand life
The places where you struggled in understanding
Is where life itself is creating new Consciousness
Find ways to shine light in the darkness of these areas of consciousness
First in yourself and then in the things you create in this world
And you align yourself with life's purpose for you!

YOU CREATE LIGHT IN THE DARKNESS

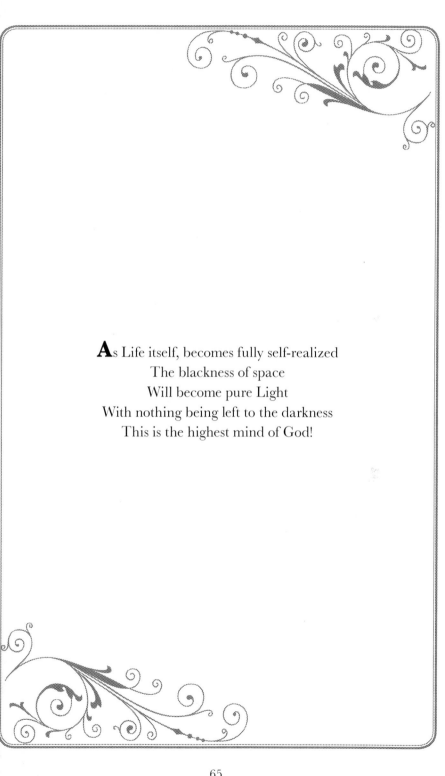

As Life itself, becomes fully self-realized
The blackness of space
Will become pure Light
With nothing being left to the darkness
This is the highest mind of God!

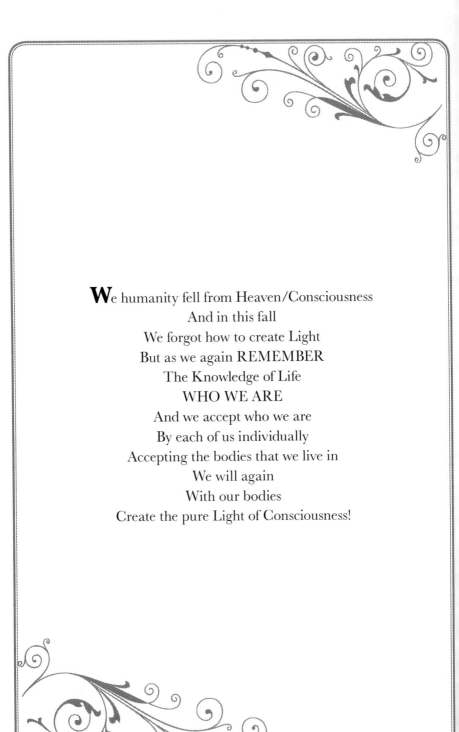

We humanity fell from Heaven/Consciousness
And in this fall
We forgot how to create Light
But as we again REMEMBER
The Knowledge of Life
WHO WE ARE
And we accept who we are
By each of us individually
Accepting the bodies that we live in
We will again
With our bodies
Create the pure Light of Consciousness!

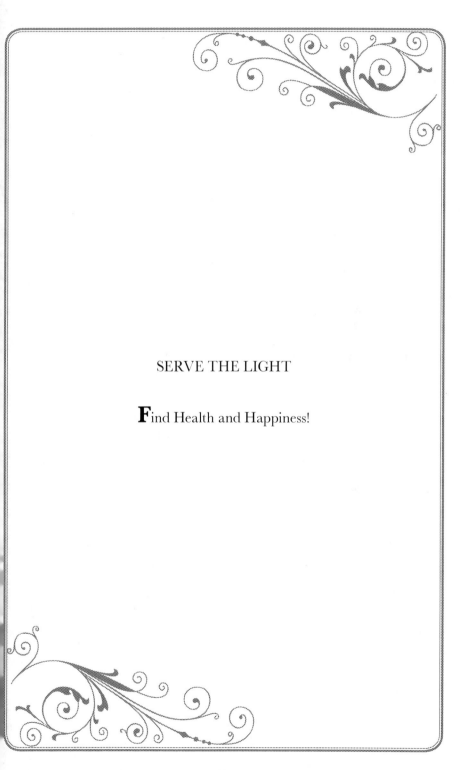

SERVE THE LIGHT

Find Health and Happiness!

We have to stop attaching negative thoughts
To the pressure we feel in our Hearts when under a stress
That overwhelming feeling that you feel in your chest
Is your Heart literally creating Fire
In an attempt to illuminate your inner world
And shine Light on the darkness
That attempts to put out your Light!

Let go of the need to be understood
The Knowledge that you have will one day
Give Light to the vastness of space

And be a STAR in the Sky!

Think about individual identity
As if it is the distance between Light and darkness
Your Consciousness (ability to see)
Grows as you move closer to the Light
And as you merge with the Light
The Consciousness of who you are
There is no more individual identity
Because there is no longer a distance
Between you and the Light
And you are then one with the Light
And have the ability to see all
Because you have merged with the Light
The Consciousness of Life itself
And you now see the Knowledge of Life
As the Creator of it… The Light itself!

To master the Energy of your Body
You first have to understand
The movement of Light
For the movement of Light
Is the energy of your Body
May your Mind, Body, and Spirit
Become one thing in understanding
Because all that exist
Is the movement of Light
Your Body now is an unbalanced Rainbow
So in balancing the Rainbow
You create a balanced movement of Light
And this then prepares you
To move in the direction
Of being able to metabolize
The higher vibrations of Light
Which then allows you to master
The Energy of your Body
As you begin to master the movements of Light!

LOVE…

Is the Light
But only until you come into the Knowledge of who you are
And then there is no Darkness
There is only Light/Love
And in that Light
All Emotions are an expression of Love!

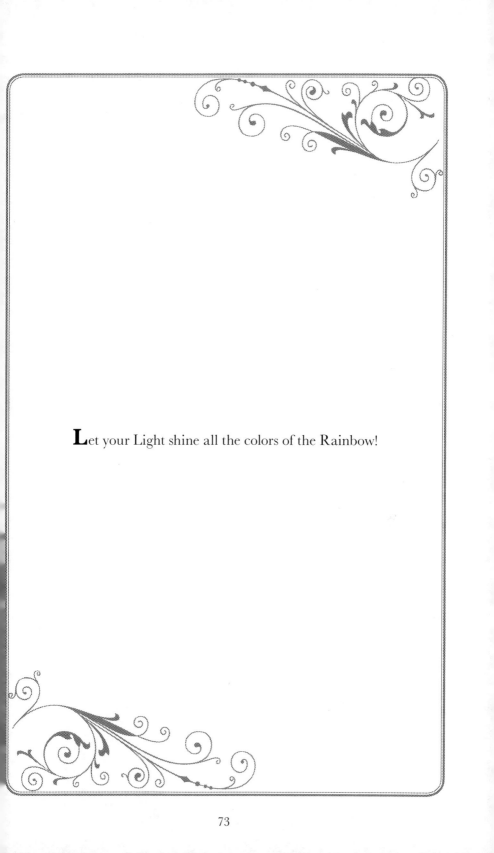

Let your Light shine all the colors of the Rainbow!

The SUN gives warmth to some
But it burns others… Be like the Sun!

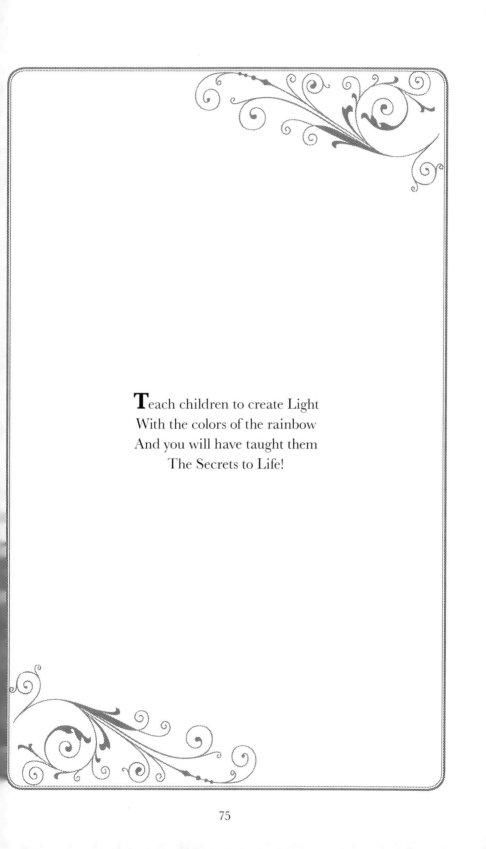

Teach children to create Light
With the colors of the rainbow
And you will have taught them
The Secrets to Life!

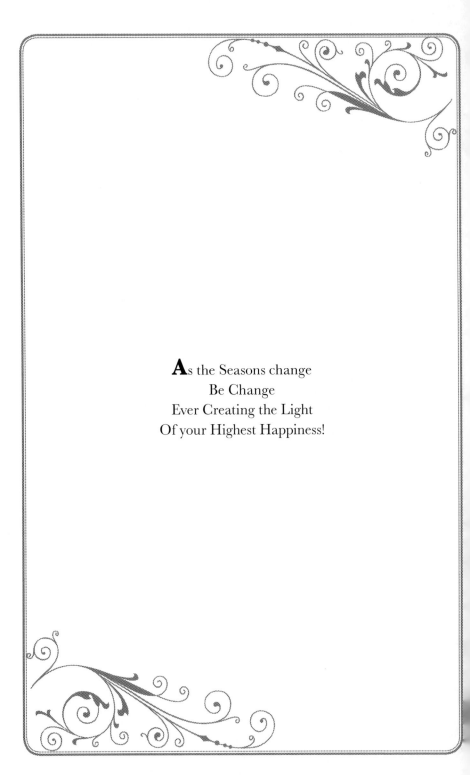

As the Seasons change
Be Change
Ever Creating the Light
Of your Highest Happiness!

Your Heartbeat speaks the vibration
Of the Energy that you metabolize
In Health this vibration is the expression of Love
And in Health this vibration creates Light
This Light then reveals to us Consciousness
It opens our EYE to see
And allows us to understand
The Knowledge of Life
This is the Knowledge of Light
And the Knowledge of Love
And the Knowledge of WHO WE ARE!

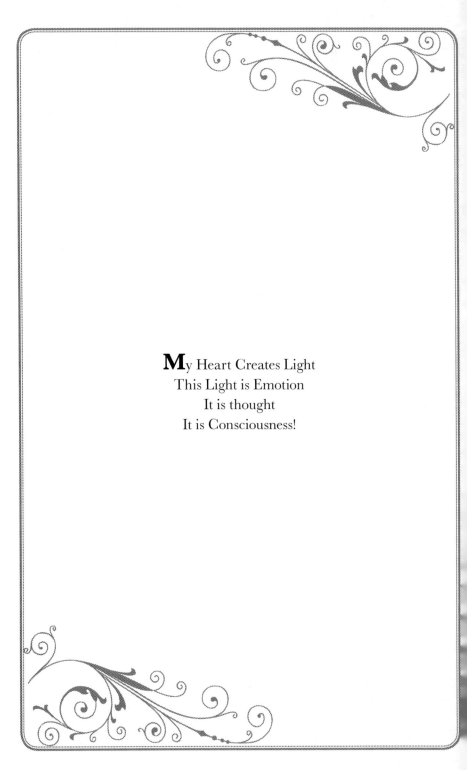

My Heart Creates Light
This Light is Emotion
It is thought
It is Consciousness!

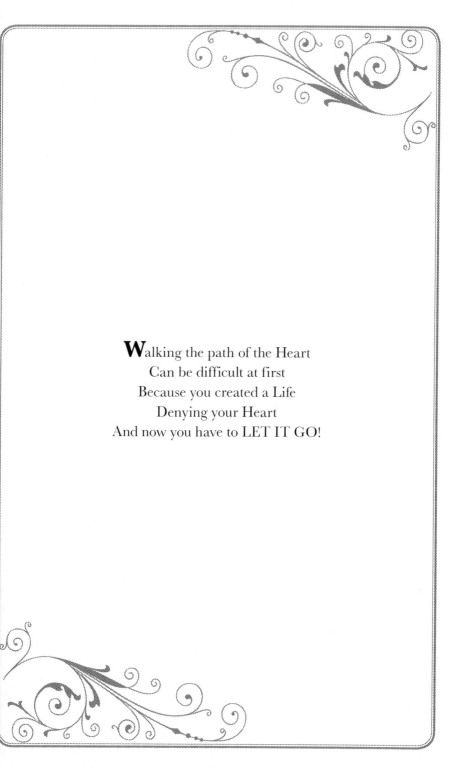

Walking the path of the Heart
Can be difficult at first
Because you created a Life
Denying your Heart
And now you have to LET IT GO!

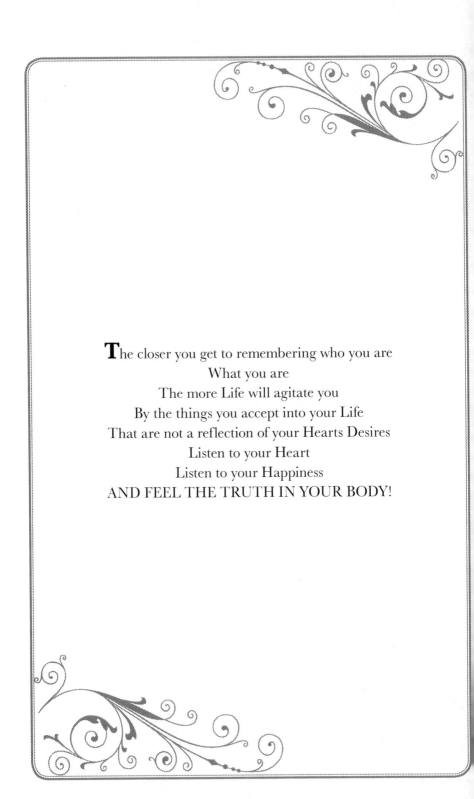

The closer you get to remembering who you are
What you are
The more Life will agitate you
By the things you accept into your Life
That are not a reflection of your Hearts Desires
Listen to your Heart
Listen to your Happiness
AND FEEL THE TRUTH IN YOUR BODY!

When first following your Heart
The opposition that you face
Doesn't mean you are going in the wrong direction
In means you built a Life
Accepting people, places, and things
That are not part of the happiness of who you are
And as you LET THESE THINGS GO
The opposition that you face
So that you can connect more
With the happiness of who you are
Is just trying to show you
That you can't bring your old Life with you!

Be malleable

But continue to move in the direction of Self Love!

LET GO

Of things that don't serve your Hearts ability to
CREATE HAPPINESS!

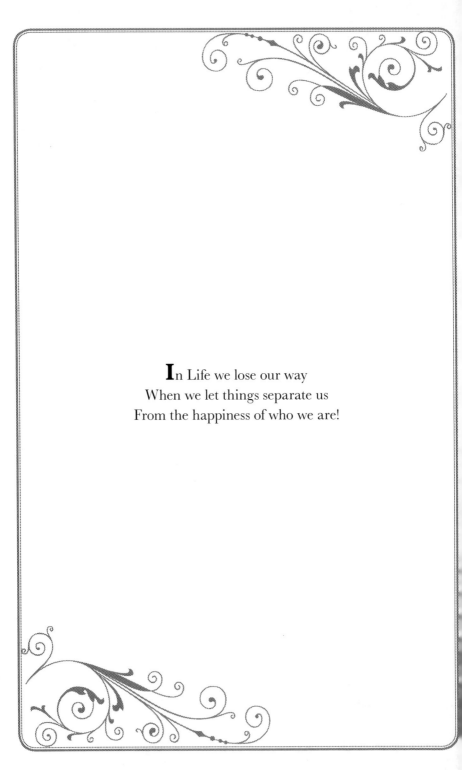

In Life we lose our way
When we let things separate us
From the happiness of who we are!

Our growth doesn't depend on our ability to face our fears
It is dependent on our ability to create
A Healthy Happy Heart
And on our ability to listen
To the desires in our Hearts
To bring those desires into creation!

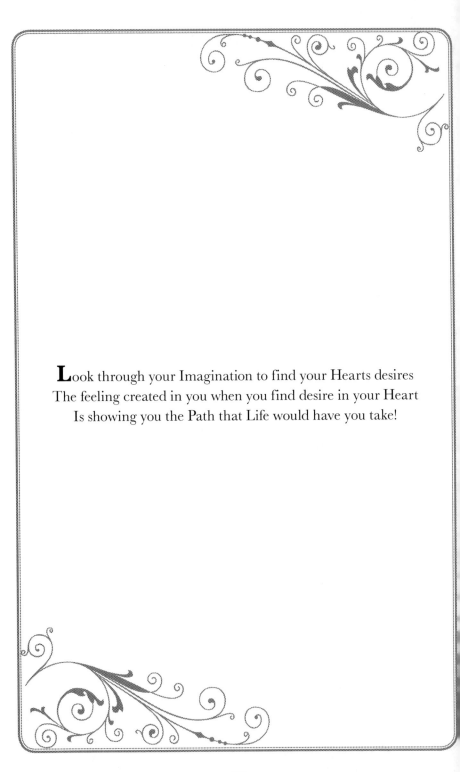

Look through your Imagination to find your Hearts desires
The feeling created in you when you find desire in your Heart
Is showing you the Path that Life would have you take!

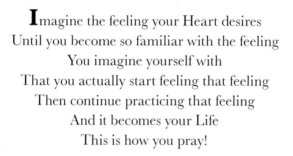

Imagine the feeling your Heart desires
Until you become so familiar with the feeling
You imagine yourself with
That you actually start feeling that feeling
Then continue practicing that feeling
And it becomes your Life
This is how you pray!

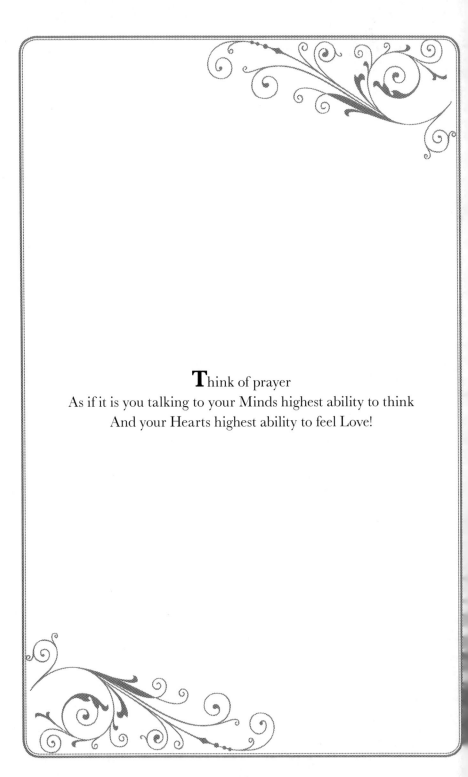

Think of prayer
As if it is you talking to your Minds highest ability to think
And your Hearts highest ability to feel Love!

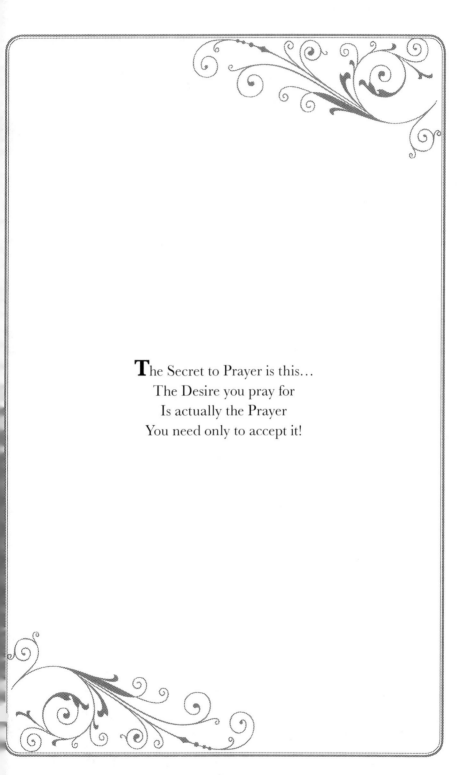

The Secret to Prayer is this…
The Desire you pray for
Is actually the Prayer
You need only to accept it!

Give yourself a Happy Heartbeat
And you create a happy Life!

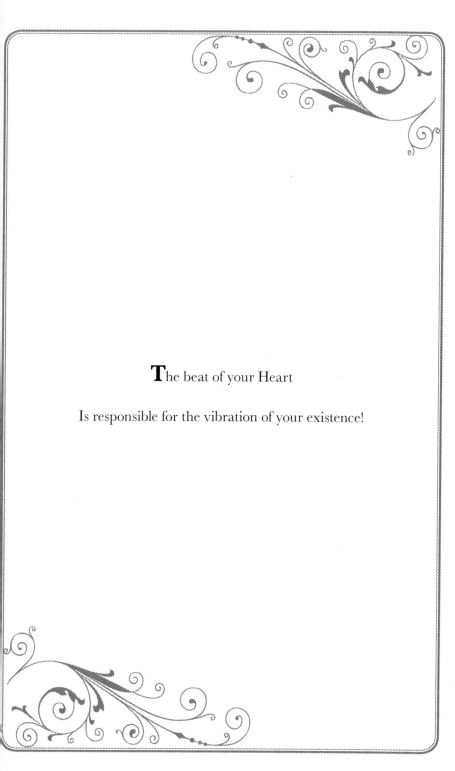

The beat of your Heart

Is responsible for the vibration of your existence!

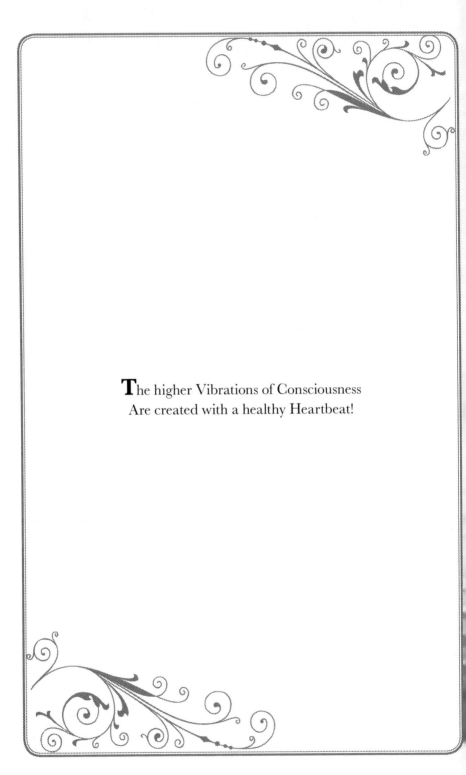

The higher Vibrations of Consciousness
Are created with a healthy Heartbeat!

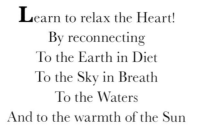

Learn to relax the Heart!
By reconnecting
To the Earth in Diet
To the Sky in Breath
To the Waters
And to the warmth of the Sun

QUESTION...

What is the highest calling of the NOW moment?

ANSWER...

To be ONE with the Earth
With the Sky
With the Water
And with the Light

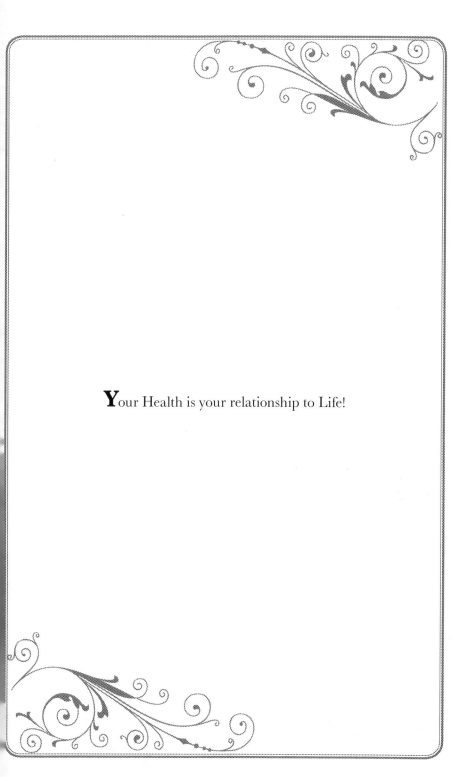

Your Health is your relationship to Life!

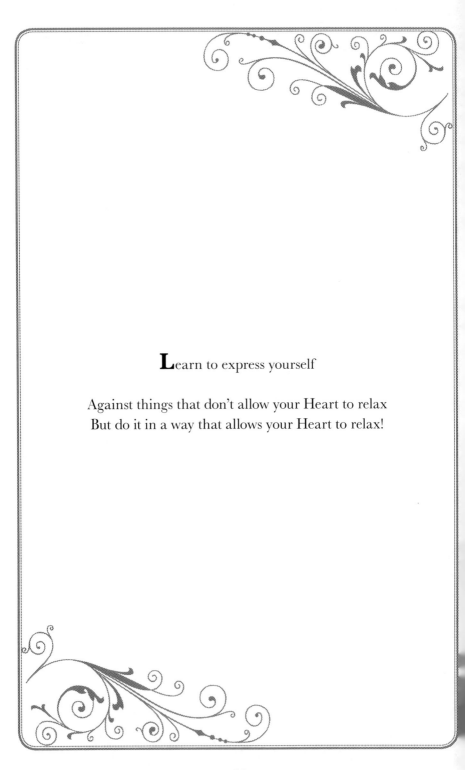

Learn to express yourself

Against things that don't allow your Heart to relax
But do it in a way that allows your Heart to relax!

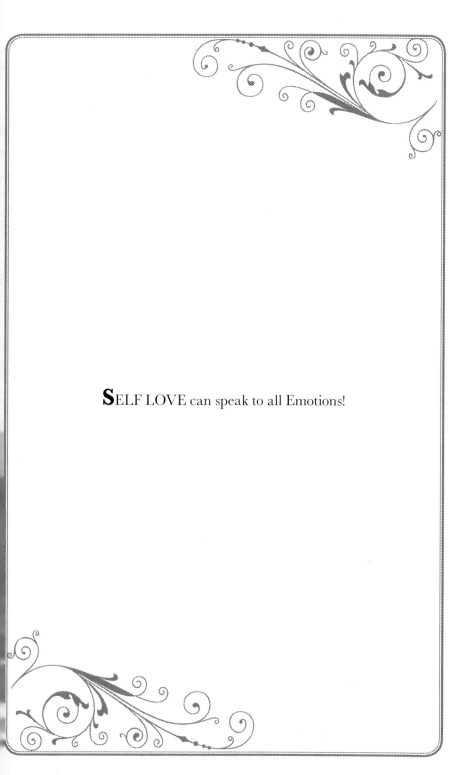

SELF LOVE can speak to all Emotions!

Happy Hearts Create Love
But unhappy Hearts deny this
So only Happy Hearts feel it!

Suffering is a thought
That says Love is absent
But the positive
And the negative
Both teach us Love!

Stop justifying the denial of your Heart
With the excuse of it being a means of your survival!

FEEL

Realize you are your Feelings
And let your feelings
Take you to your Happiness!

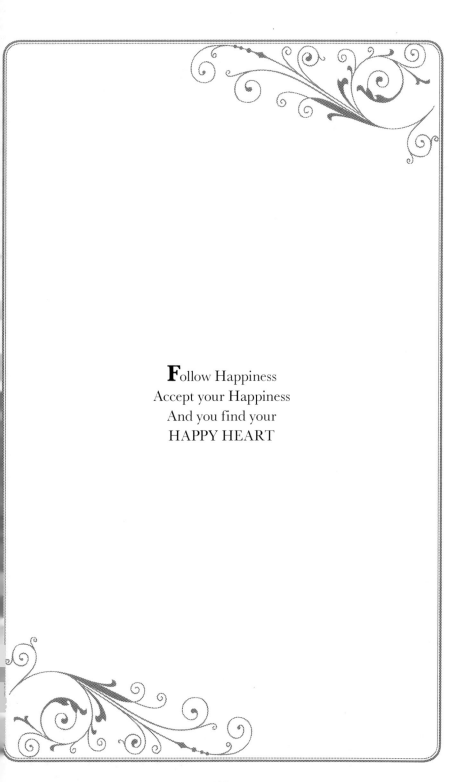

Follow Happiness
Accept your Happiness
And you find your
HAPPY HEART

HAPPINESS feels so good
Because it's WHO YOU ARE!

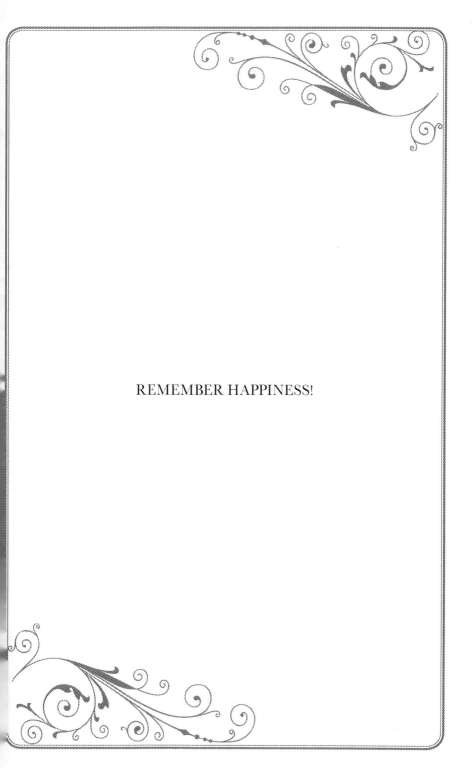

REMEMBER HAPPINESS!

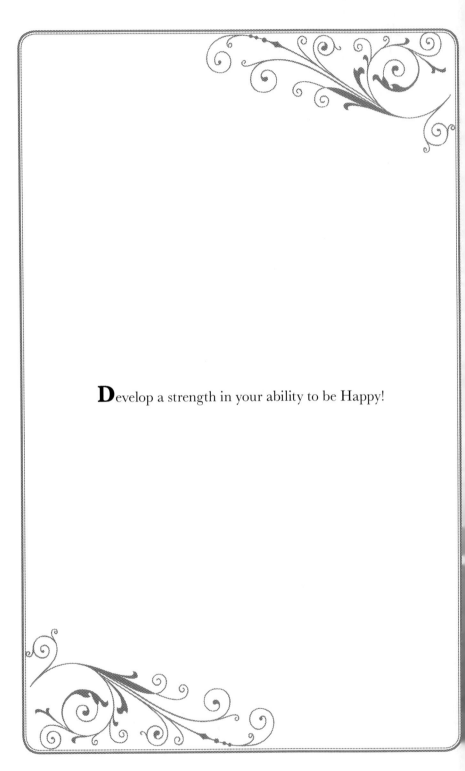

Develop a strength in your ability to be Happy!

It's not about learning
To be happy in all situations
Or accepting your unhappiness
It's about accepting yourself
And following your Heart!

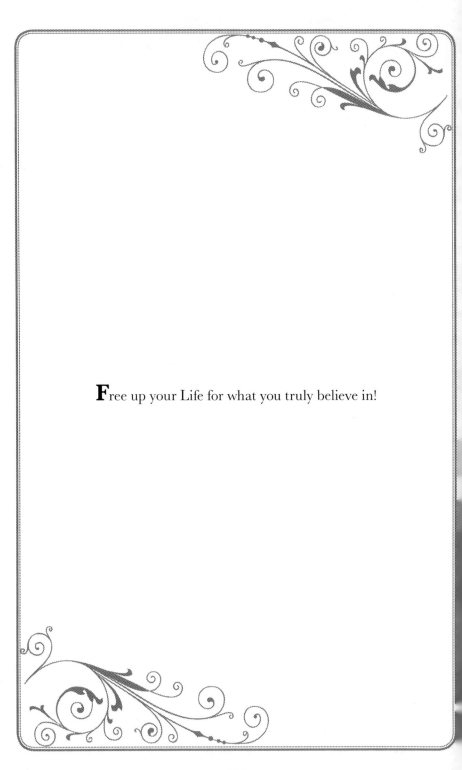

Free up your Life for what you truly believe in!

Find again the feeling of Freedom you were born with!

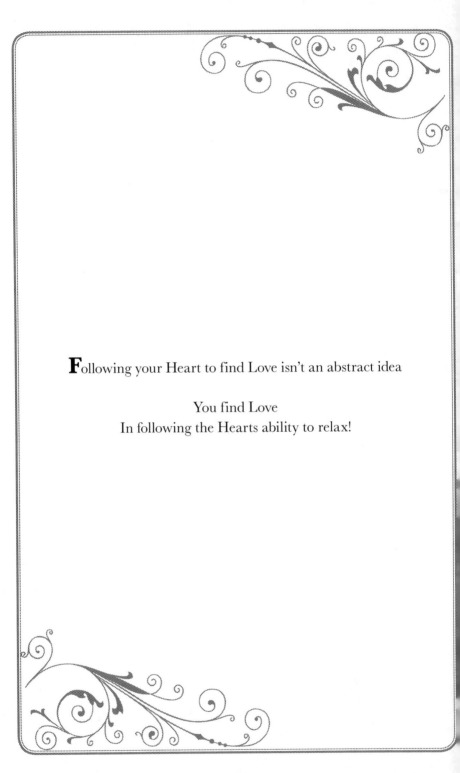

Following your Heart to find Love isn't an abstract idea

You find Love
In following the Hearts ability to relax!

Life changing affirmation

I AM a Heart
My beat moves without restriction and I vibrate Love!

Be a Happy Heart!

I love to get up first thing in the morning
So I can go outside
And Sunbath, Meditate, and do mantras…
BUTT NAKED
It's so freeing
YOU SHOULD TRY IT!
☺

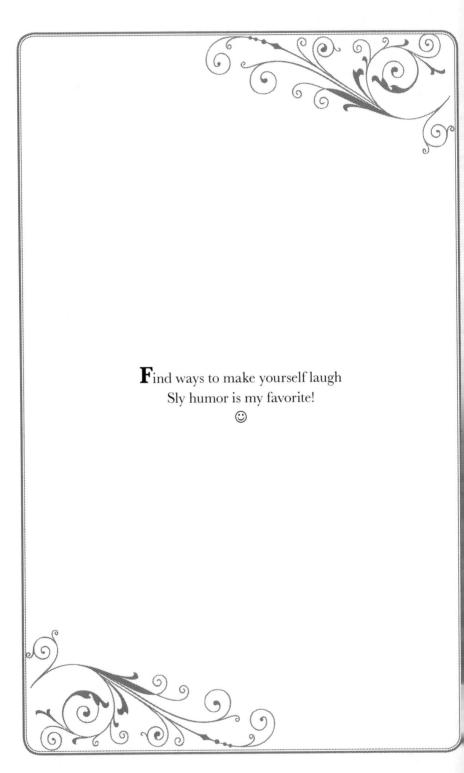

Find ways to make yourself laugh
Sly humor is my favorite!
☺

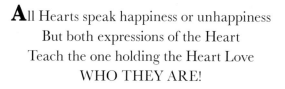

All Hearts speak happiness or unhappiness
But both expressions of the Heart
Teach the one holding the Heart Love
WHO THEY ARE!

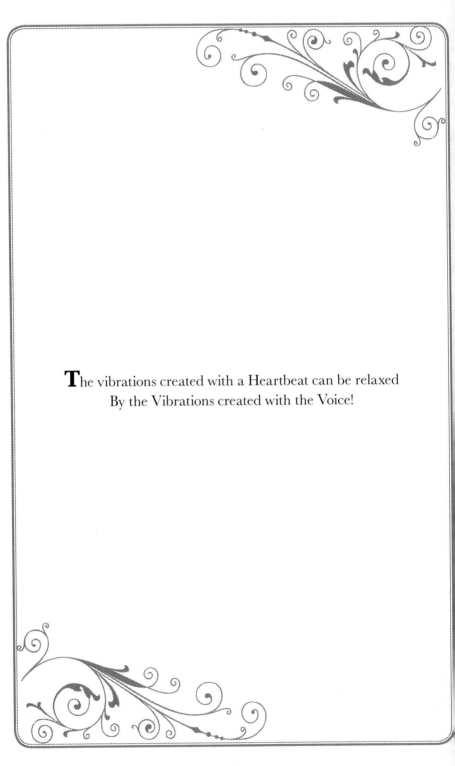

The vibrations created with a Heartbeat can be relaxed
By the Vibrations created with the Voice!

The body's ability to create Sound
Can be used in two ways
To move energy outside of the body
And to move energy inside of the body
I say this so that you can learn
To create Consciousness without word
Using just the Sounds of your Voice!

With your attention…

Follow Sound into the Body
Into the Thought
And into Emotion!

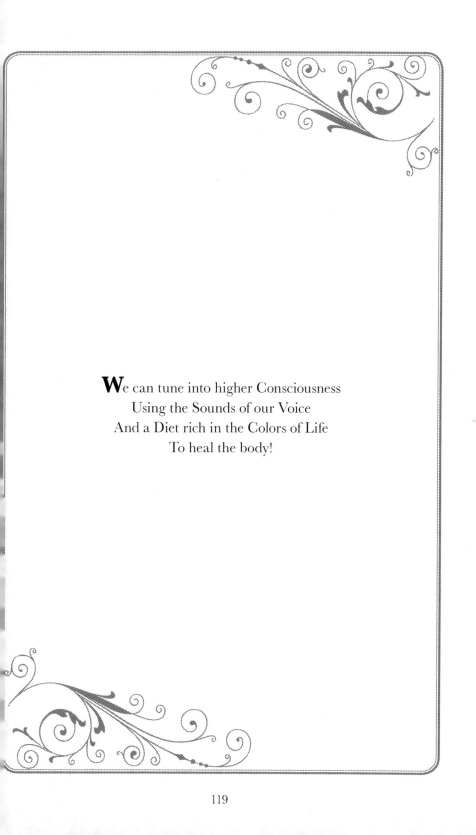

We can tune into higher Consciousness
Using the Sounds of our Voice
And a Diet rich in the Colors of Life
To heal the body!

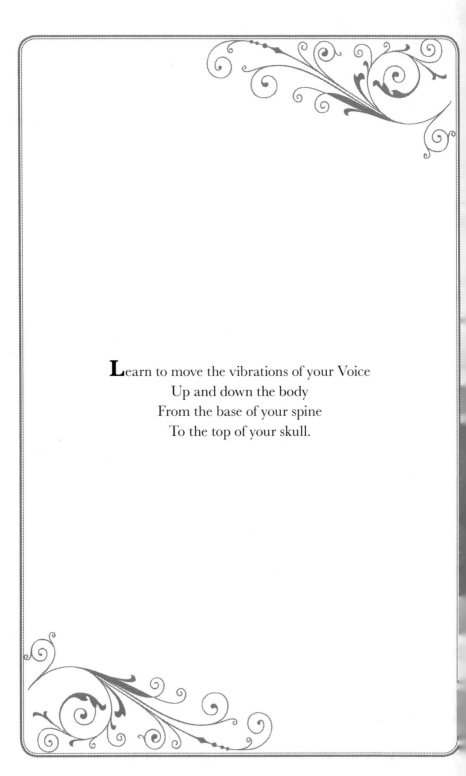

Learn to move the vibrations of your Voice
Up and down the body
From the base of your spine
To the top of your skull.

Teach yourself how all Sound can come together
To create one pure Sound
This is the Sound of White Light
Your Highest Consciousness!

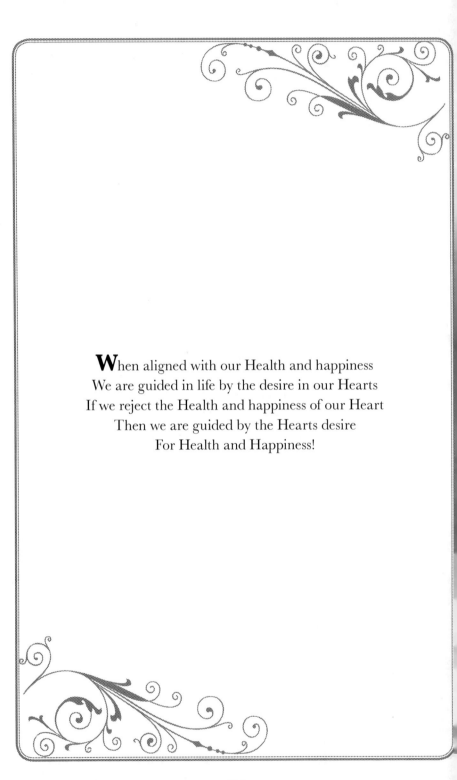

When aligned with our Health and happiness
We are guided in life by the desire in our Hearts
If we reject the Health and happiness of our Heart
Then we are guided by the Hearts desire
For Health and Happiness!

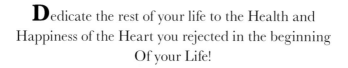

Dedicate the rest of your life to the Health and
Happiness of the Heart you rejected in the beginning
Of your Life!

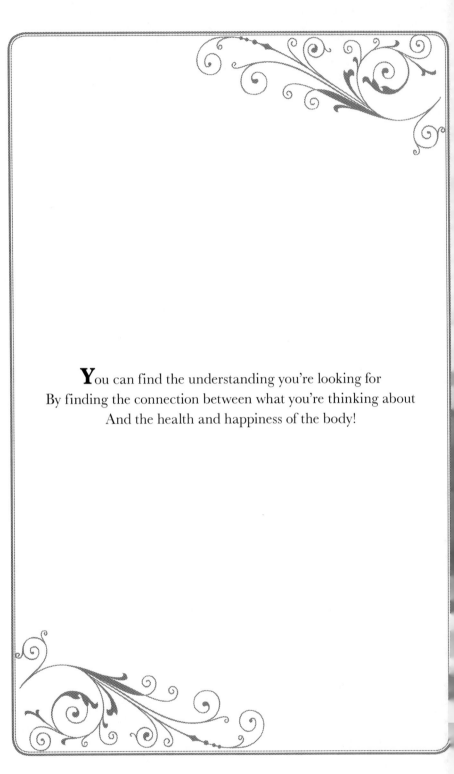

You can find the understanding you're looking for
By finding the connection between what you're thinking about
And the health and happiness of the body!

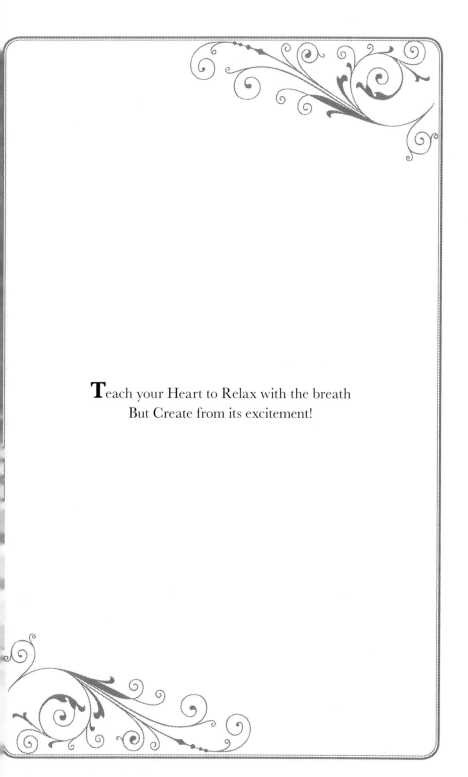

Teach your Heart to Relax with the breath
But Create from its excitement!

Take a Heart breath!

Live Life as a Heart that Breathes!

Next time you hug a loved one
Try and Feel their Heartbeat!

Faith in Life is Faith in yourself
And the proof this is the true Faith
Is the Happiness it creates in the Body
And the Love it creates in your Heart!

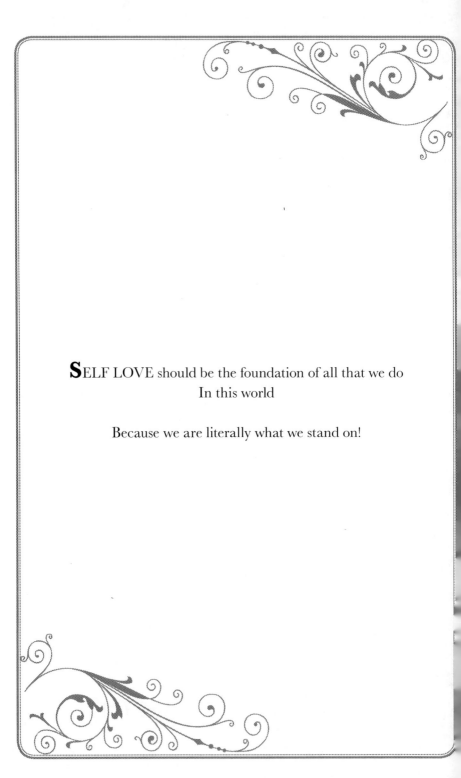

SELF LOVE should be the foundation of all that we do
In this world

Because we are literally what we stand on!

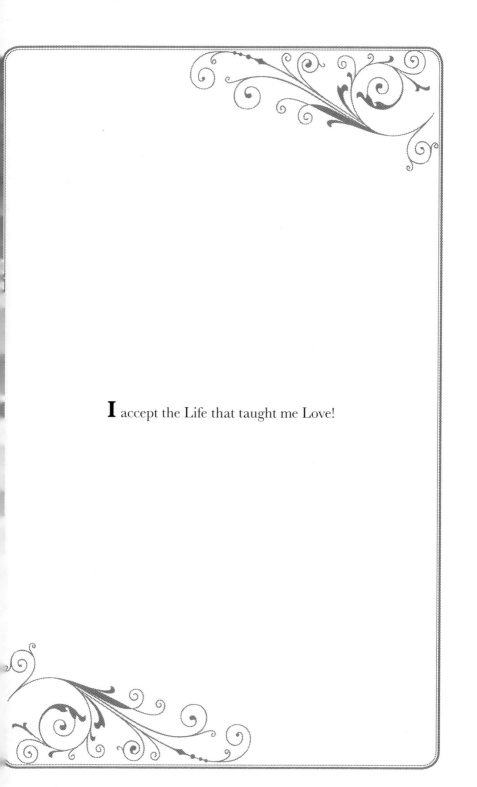

I accept the Life that taught me Love!

Believe in Life!

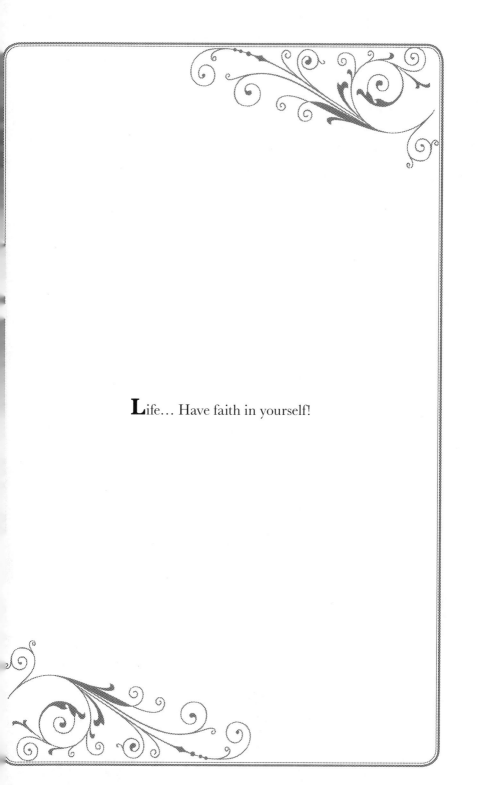

Life… Have faith in yourself!

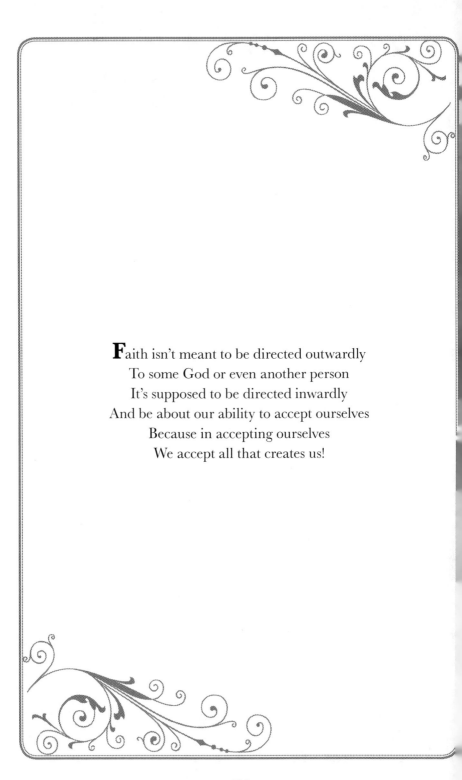

Faith isn't meant to be directed outwardly
To some God or even another person
It's supposed to be directed inwardly
And be about our ability to accept ourselves
Because in accepting ourselves
We accept all that creates us!

I AM LIFE

So Life is my desire
And I find the ability to ACCEPT MYSELF
TO ACCEPT LIFE
When I support what allows me to continue
My Health and my Happiness!

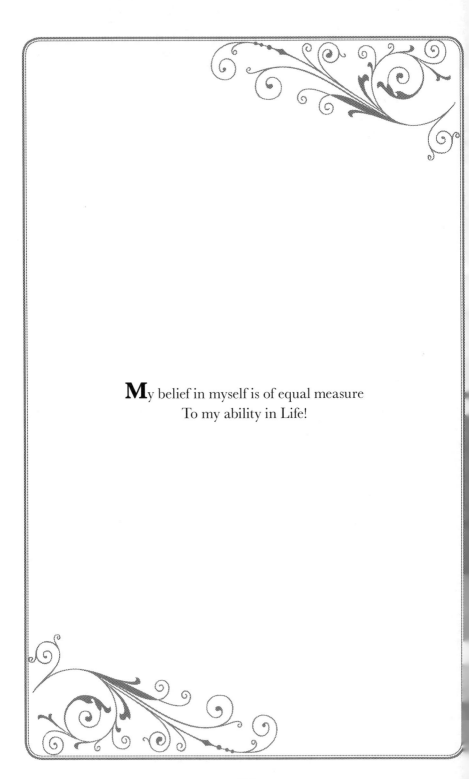

My belief in myself is of equal measure
To my ability in Life!

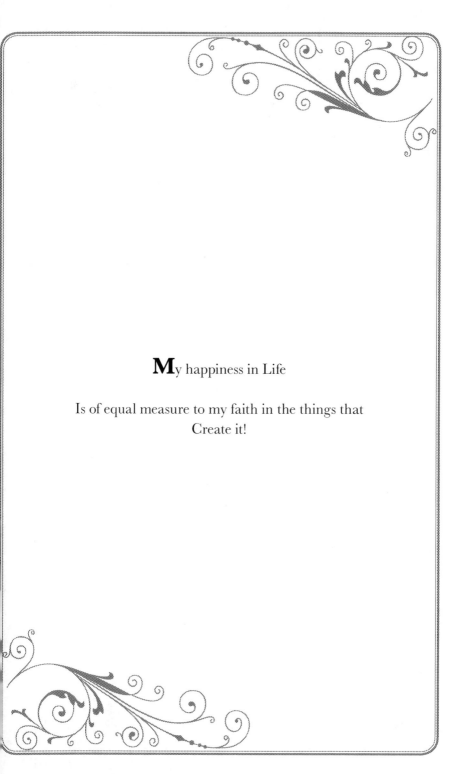

My happiness in Life

Is of equal measure to my faith in the things that
Create it!

The
Faith
That saves us is a faith in the body we live in
Can you see how Faith in yourself
Is
Faith
In
The
Life
That
Surrounds
You?

What is your body made of?

I have Faith in…

The Earth, the Sky, the Water, and the Light
Because it's what I AM!

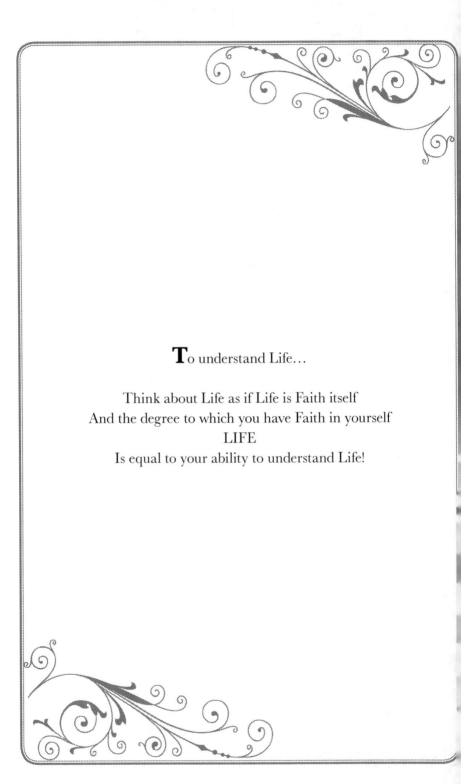

To understand Life…

Think about Life as if Life is Faith itself
And the degree to which you have Faith in yourself
LIFE
Is equal to your ability to understand Life!

You will GROW your THOUGHTS and EVOLVE your
CONSCIOUSNESS
When you grow your thoughts the same way the Earth
Creates Life
With the Air, with the Water, and with the Light!

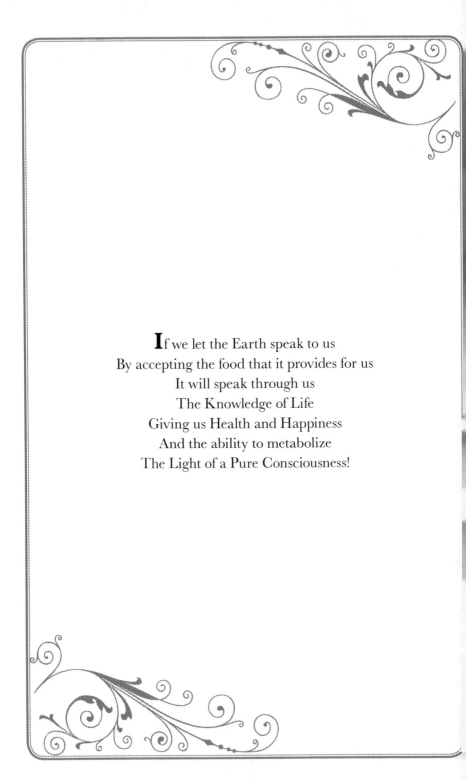

If we let the Earth speak to us
By accepting the food that it provides for us
It will speak through us
The Knowledge of Life
Giving us Health and Happiness
And the ability to metabolize
The Light of a Pure Consciousness!

EAT THE COLORS OF THE RAINBOW IN EVERY MEAL
As you do this your Body better develops the ability

TO CREATE LIGHT!

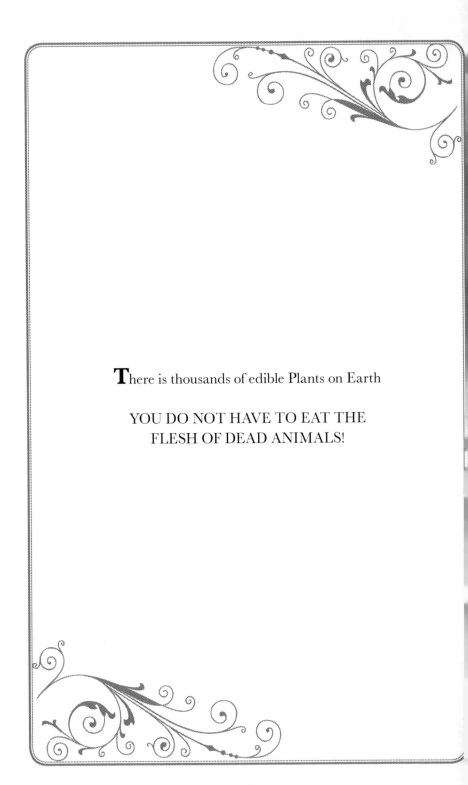

There is thousands of edible Plants on Earth

YOU DO NOT HAVE TO EAT THE
FLESH OF DEAD ANIMALS!

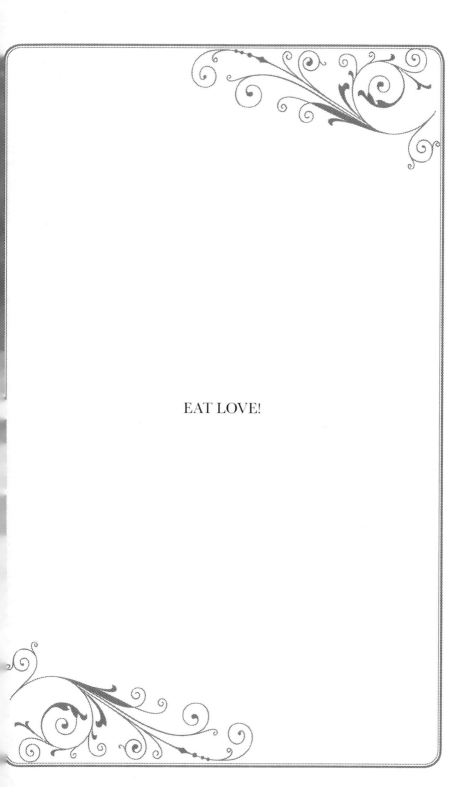

EAT LOVE!

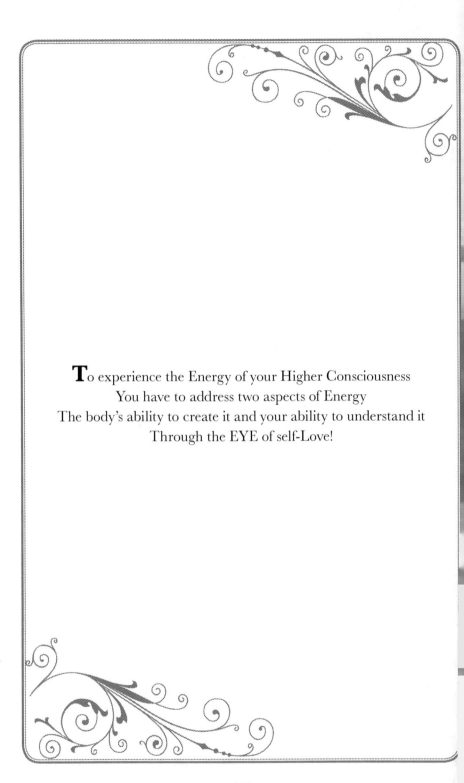

To experience the Energy of your Higher Consciousness
You have to address two aspects of Energy
The body's ability to create it and your ability to understand it
Through the EYE of self-Love!

Breath in the Sky

Let it to open your Mind and open your Heart!

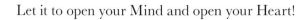

Let the Earth give you Food
And Awareness of Life!

Flow like the Waters

And restrict not the Flow of Energy through your Body
So you can move through the Awareness of this Life with Grace!

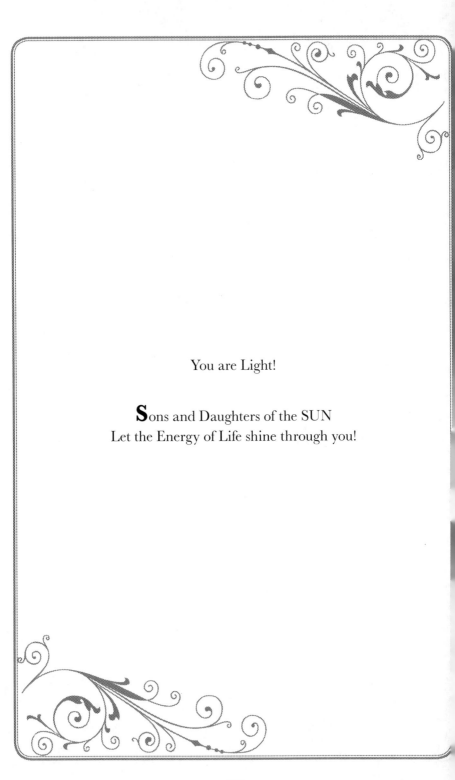

You are Light!

Sons and Daughters of the SUN
Let the Energy of Life shine through you!

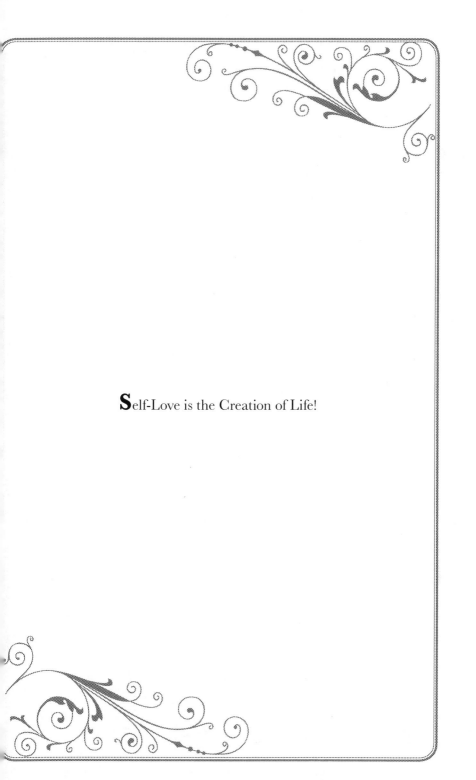

Self-Love is the Creation of Life!

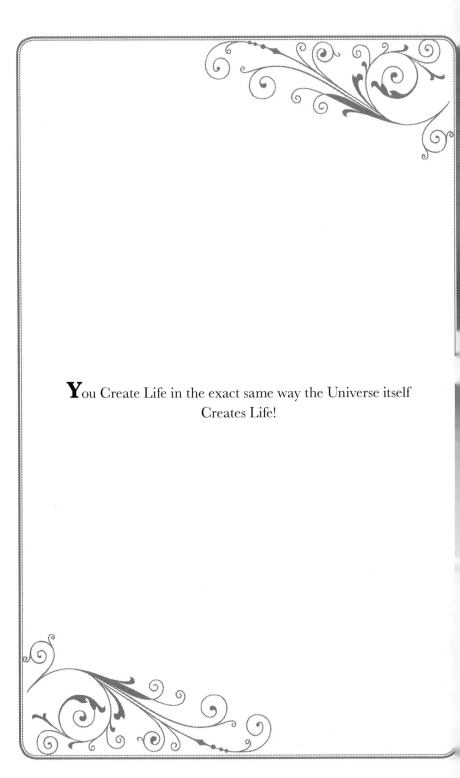

You Create Life in the exact same way the Universe itself Creates Life!

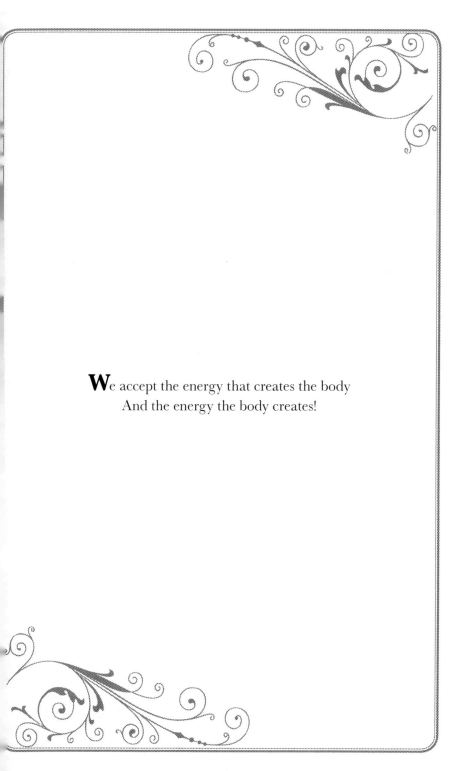

We accept the energy that creates the body
And the energy the body creates!

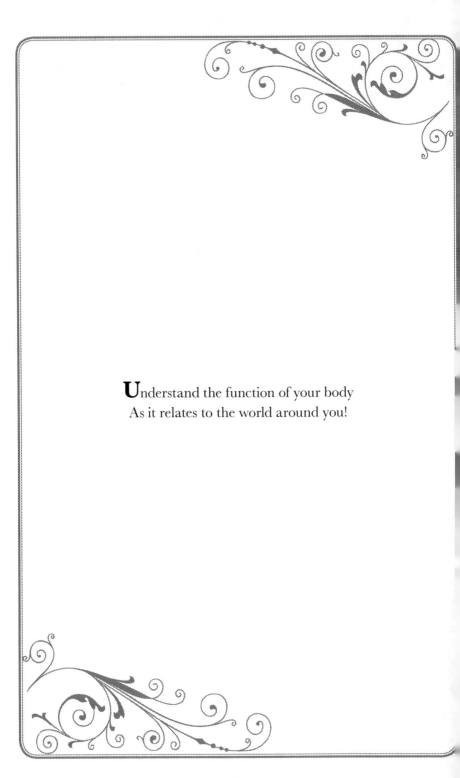

Understand the function of your body
As it relates to the world around you!

The energy you take in through all five of your senses
Becomes your body's emotion.

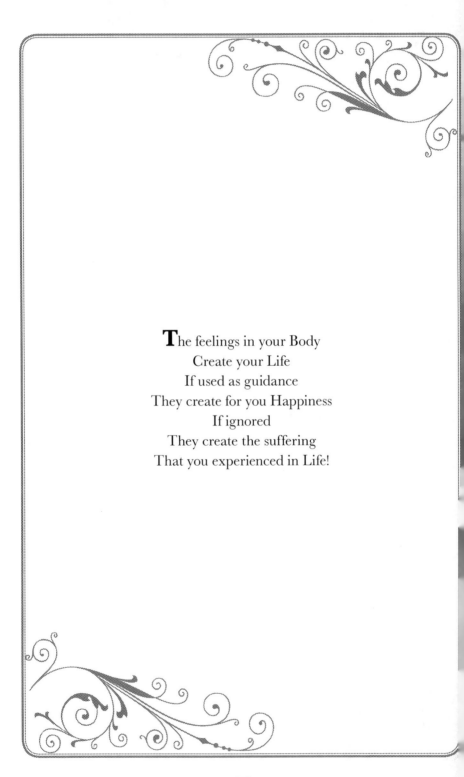

The feelings in your Body
Create your Life
If used as guidance
They create for you Happiness
If ignored
They create the suffering
That you experienced in Life!

The Feelings you feel and the Thoughts you think
IS the Mind and Body
Vibrating the Energy
That you receive through your five senses
From the World around you
Inside of your Mind and Body

THINK ABOUT THAT FOR A MINUTE!

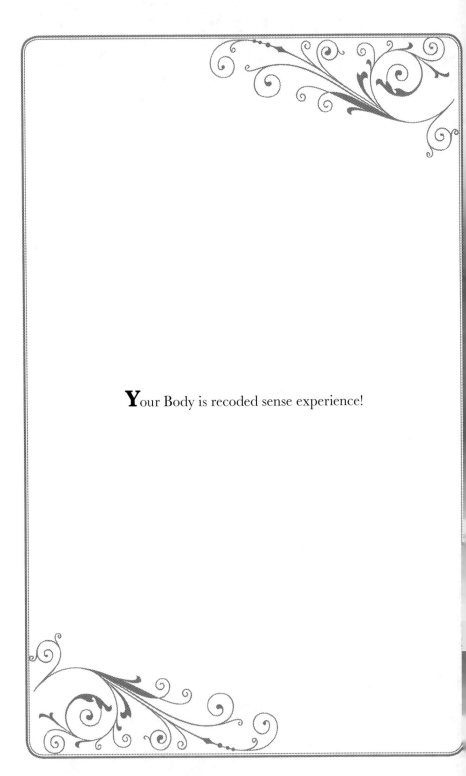

Your Body is recoded sense experience!

If we consume only Health and Happiness
To the best of our ability

We will then be able to Create Health and Happiness
To the best of our ability!

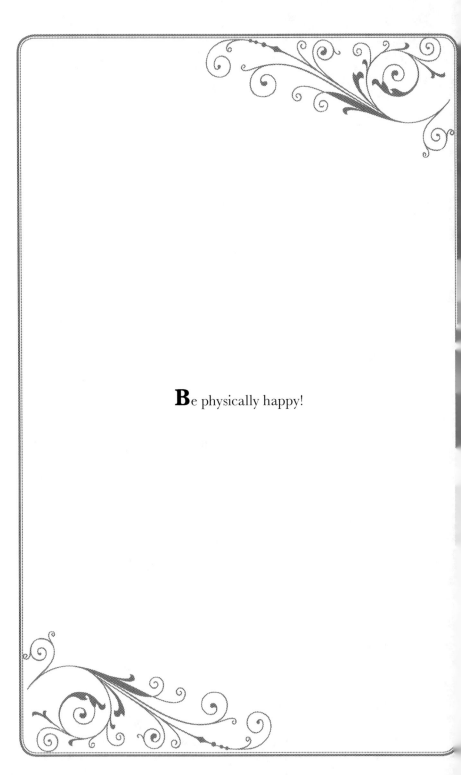

Be physically happy!

The ups and downs we experience emotionally
Is just the body's ability or Inability to create Energy!

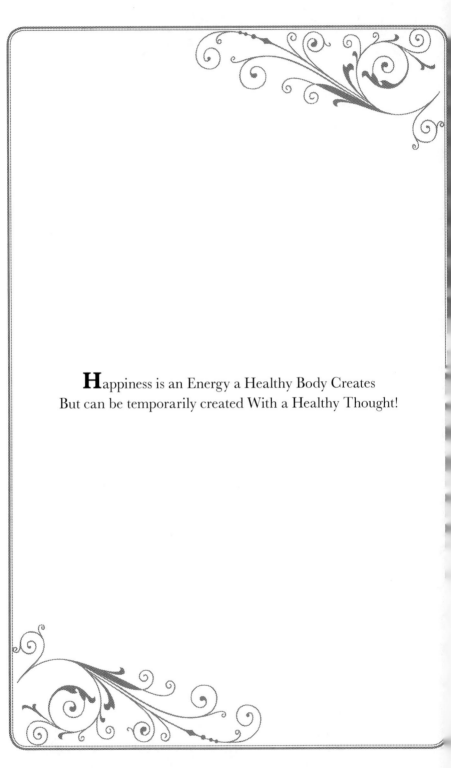

Happiness is an Energy a Healthy Body Creates
But can be temporarily created With a Healthy Thought!

Figure out how to Love yourself in thought... Yes!
It's good to create that Energy inside yourself
But don't forget that a healthy body creates energy!

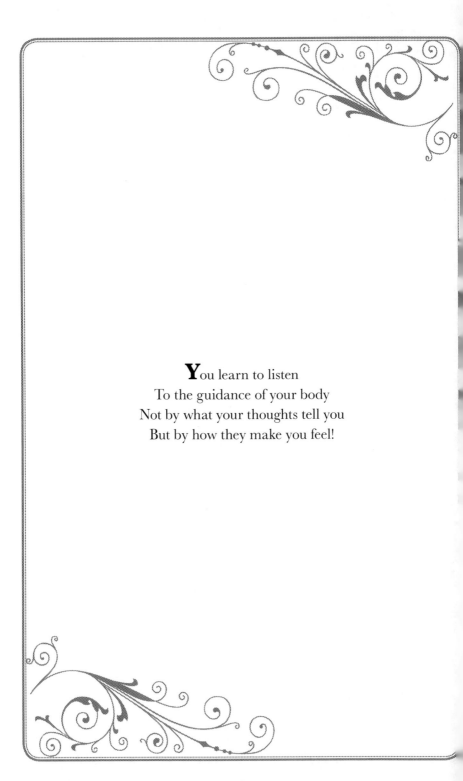

You learn to listen
To the guidance of your body
Not by what your thoughts tell you
But by how they make you feel!

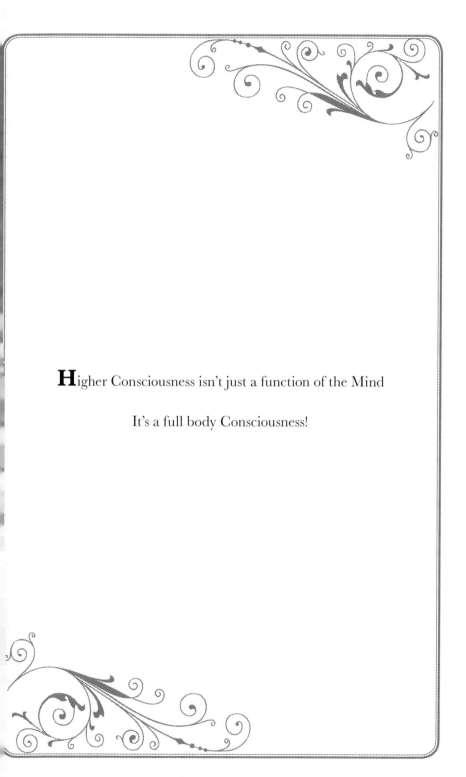

Higher Consciousness isn't just a function of the Mind

It's a full body Consciousness!

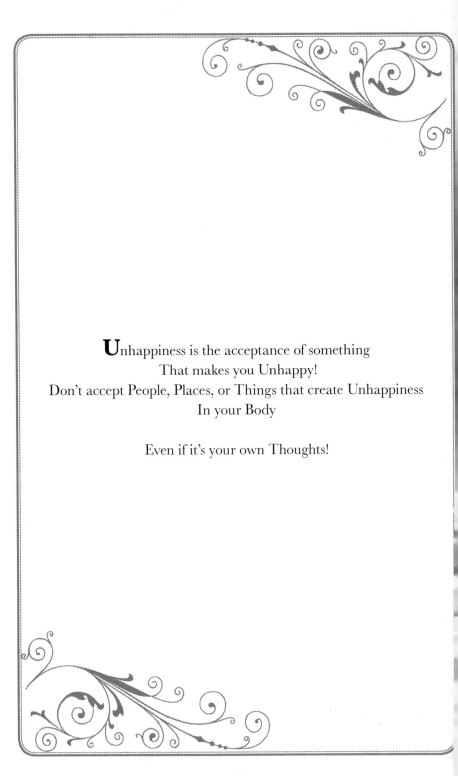

Unhappiness is the acceptance of something
That makes you Unhappy!
Don't accept People, Places, or Things that create Unhappiness
In your Body

Even if it's your own Thoughts!

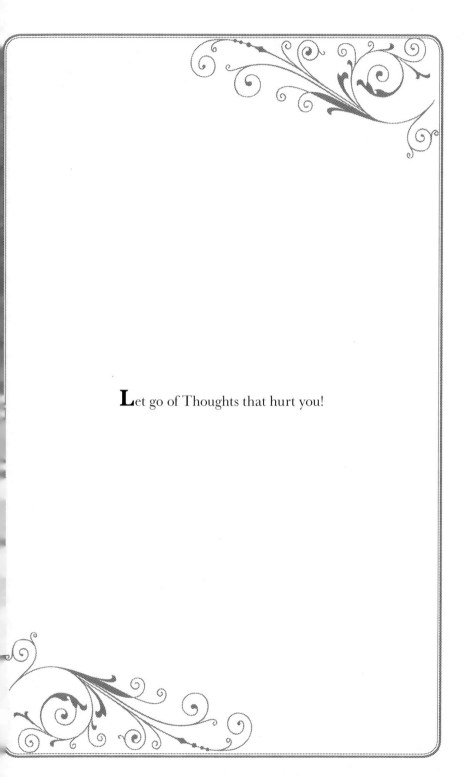

Let go of Thoughts that hurt you!

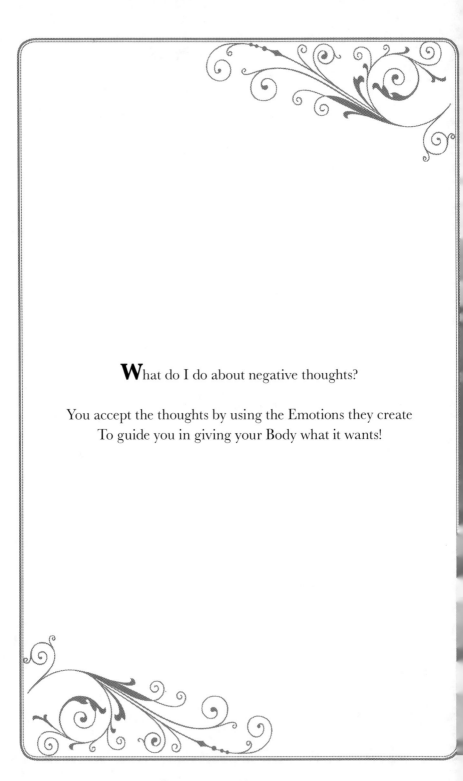

What do I do about negative thoughts?

You accept the thoughts by using the Emotions they create
To guide you in giving your Body what it wants!

Unhappiness isn't something we change
It's something that shows us
That we need change!

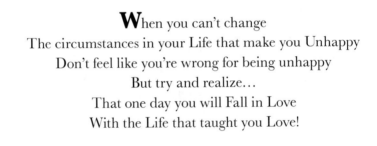

When you can't change
The circumstances in your Life that make you Unhappy
Don't feel like you're wrong for being unhappy
But try and realize…
That one day you will Fall in Love
With the Life that taught you Love!

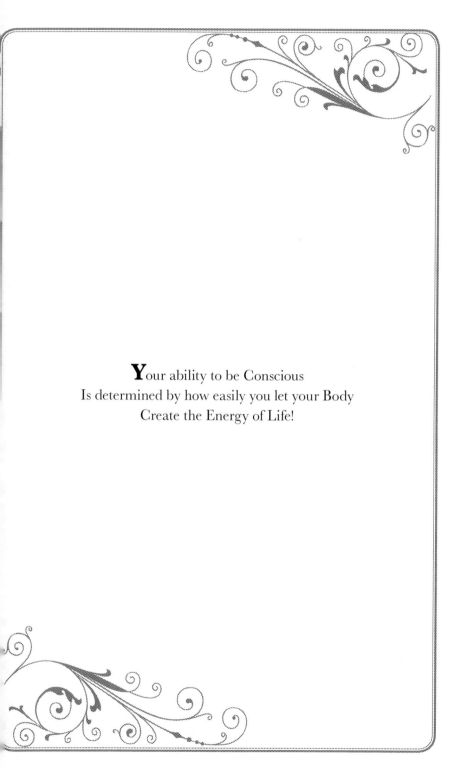

Your ability to be Conscious
Is determined by how easily you let your Body
Create the Energy of Life!

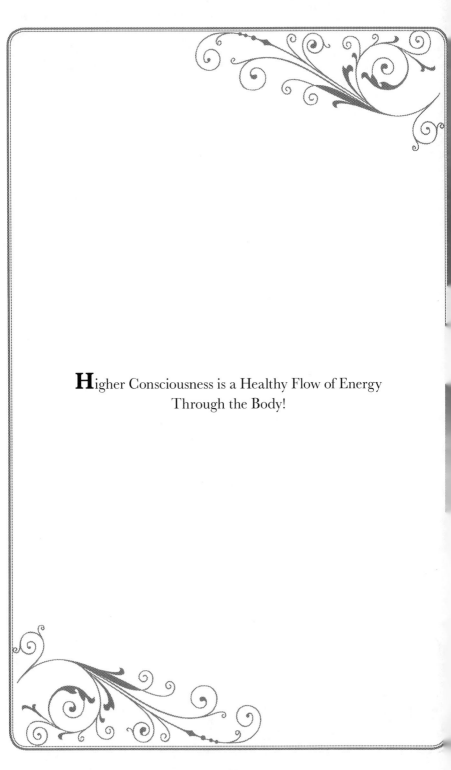

Higher Consciousness is a Healthy Flow of Energy
Through the Body!

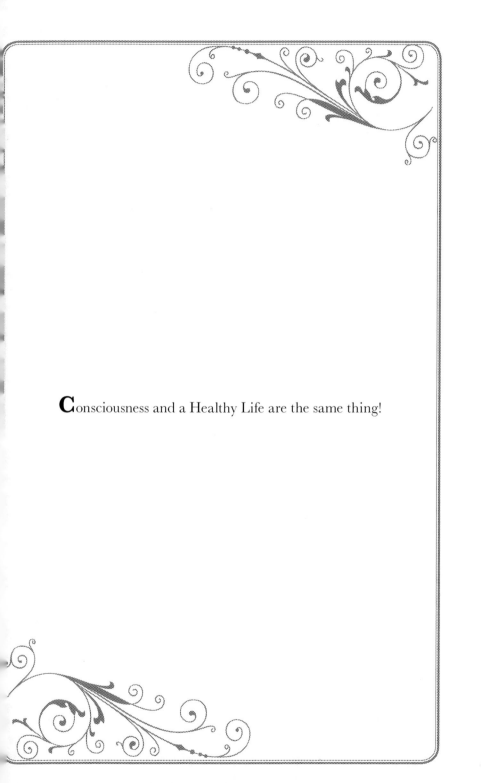

Consciousness and a Healthy Life are the same thing!

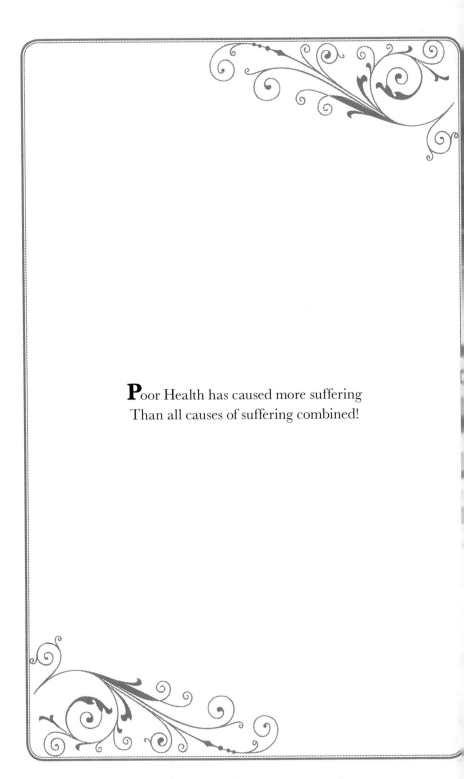

Poor Health has caused more suffering
Than all causes of suffering combined!

The World has struggled
To rise above the Consciousness that creates suffering
Because having the Health of Life to end Suffering
Is the Consciousness that ends suffering!

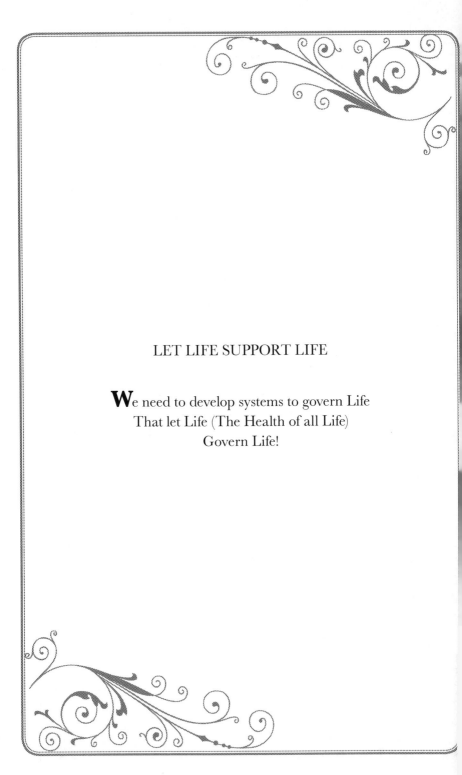

LET LIFE SUPPORT LIFE

We need to develop systems to govern Life
That let Life (The Health of all Life)
Govern Life!

The Function of a city will be the Growth of a Garden!

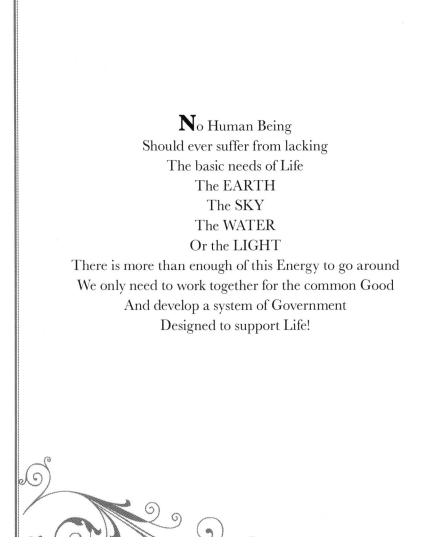

No Human Being
Should ever suffer from lacking
The basic needs of Life
The EARTH
The SKY
The WATER
Or the LIGHT
There is more than enough of this Energy to go around
We only need to work together for the common Good
And develop a system of Government
Designed to support Life!

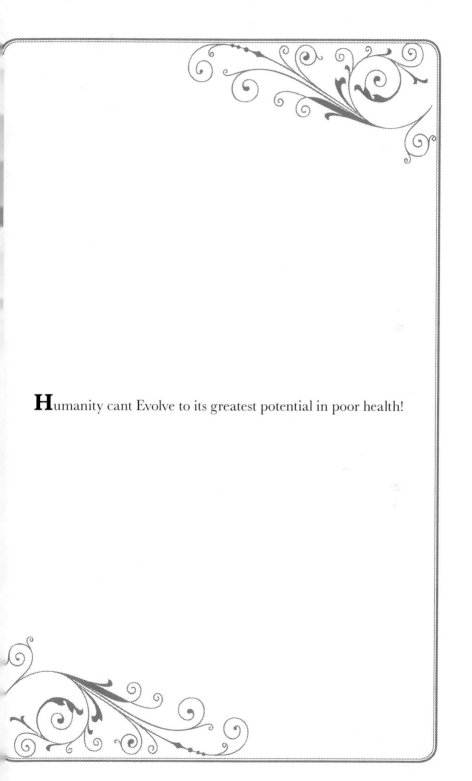

Humanity cant Evolve to its greatest potential in poor health!

AFFIRMATOION FOR A BETTER WORLD

I made a lasting difference
In the World
For the Health and Happiness of the Planet
And Evolved
The experience of Human Life
To move humanity further
Into the Evolution
Of our Enlightenment
So we would again
Find our Highest Happiness
And REMEMBER…
The Knowledge of Who We Are!

Your Passion to save the World
May first have to be used to save you
From the world you created for yourself
Denying your Heart!

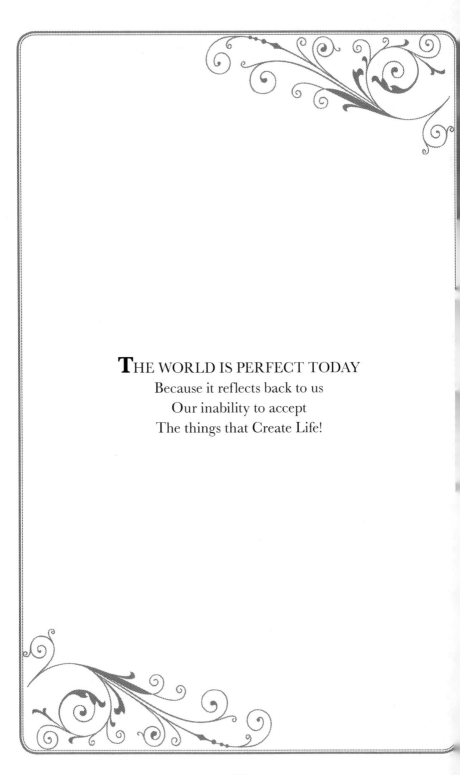

THE WORLD IS PERFECT TODAY
Because it reflects back to us
Our inability to accept
The things that Create Life!

We change the World one accepted Heart at a time
And we start first with the Heart that we hold!

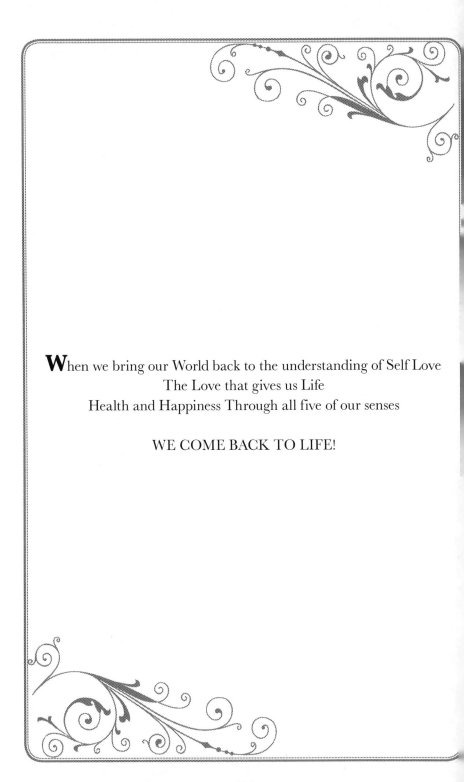

When we bring our World back to the understanding of Self Love
The Love that gives us Life
Health and Happiness Through all five of our senses

WE COME BACK TO LIFE!

To understand
Unconditional Love
Stop thinking about it
As if it is something
You have to give
To the world around you
And think about it
As if it is a Love
You give to yourself!

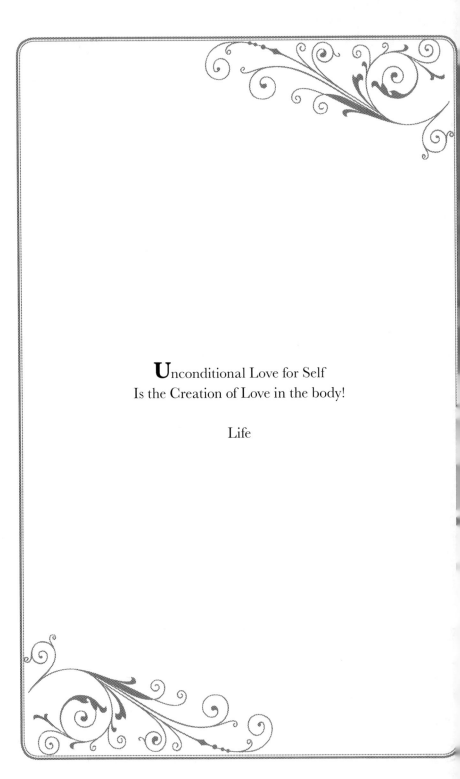

Unconditional Love for Self
Is the Creation of Love in the body!

Life

LOVE

Is not a choice
Why do you pretend to Love?
Love is what the body is
If you accept it
It's Health and its Happiness
You cannot choose Love
You can only choose
To reject Love!

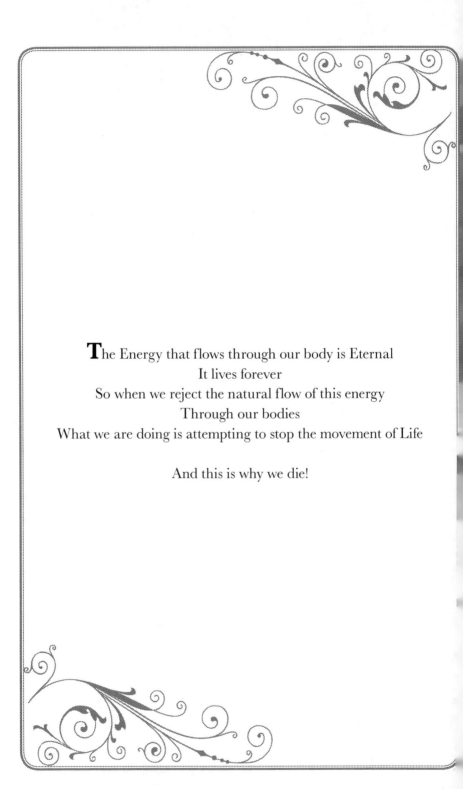

The Energy that flows through our body is Eternal
It lives forever
So when we reject the natural flow of this energy
Through our bodies
What we are doing is attempting to stop the movement of Life

And this is why we die!

LIFE is Life's guide!

And the body's desire for health and happiness
Is how it speaks to us!

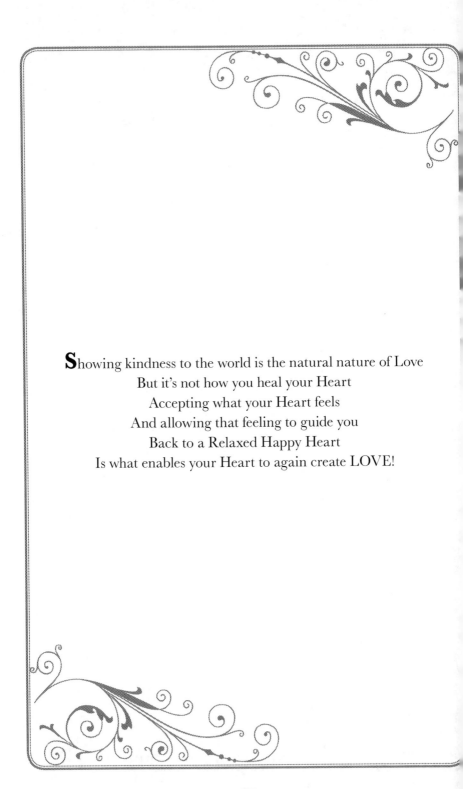

Showing kindness to the world is the natural nature of Love
But it's not how you heal your Heart
Accepting what your Heart feels
And allowing that feeling to guide you
Back to a Relaxed Happy Heart
Is what enables your Heart to again create LOVE!

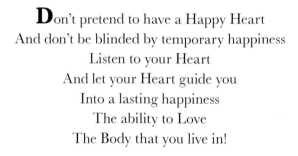

Don't pretend to have a Happy Heart
And don't be blinded by temporary happiness
Listen to your Heart
And let your Heart guide you
Into a lasting happiness
The ability to Love
The Body that you live in!

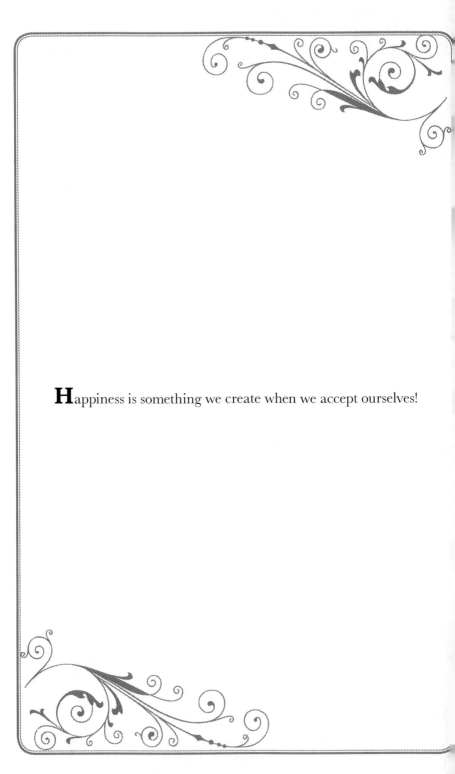

Happiness is something we create when we accept ourselves!

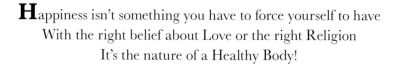

Happiness isn't something you have to force yourself to have
With the right belief about Love or the right Religion
It's the nature of a Healthy Body!

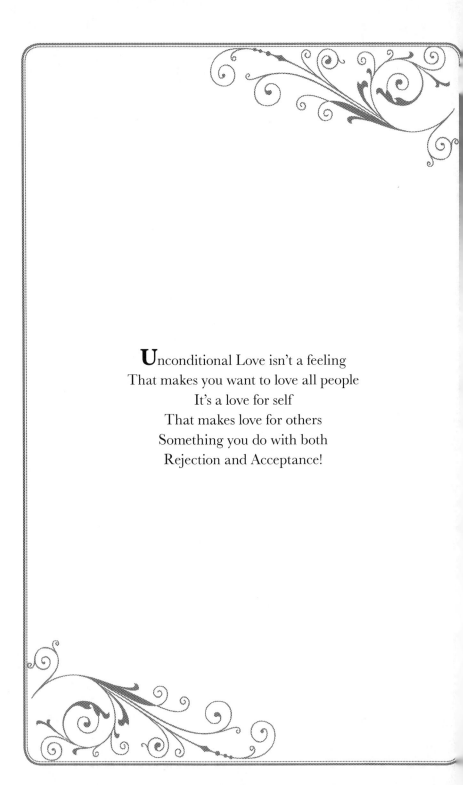

Unconditional Love isn't a feeling
That makes you want to love all people
It's a love for self
That makes love for others
Something you do with both
Rejection and Acceptance!

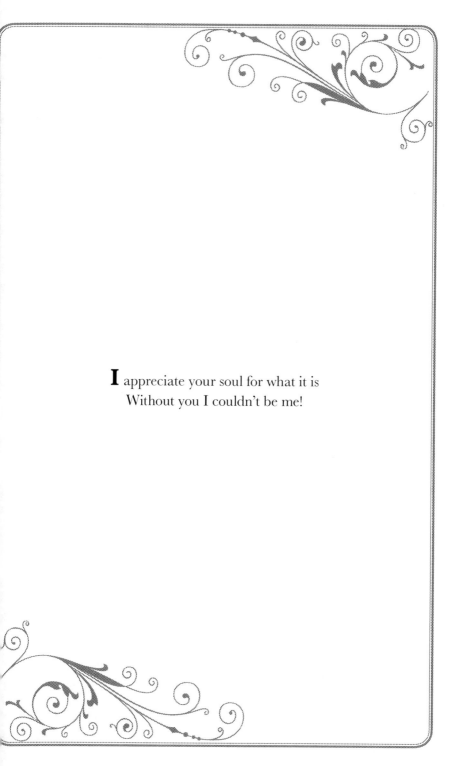

I appreciate your soul for what it is
Without you I couldn't be me!

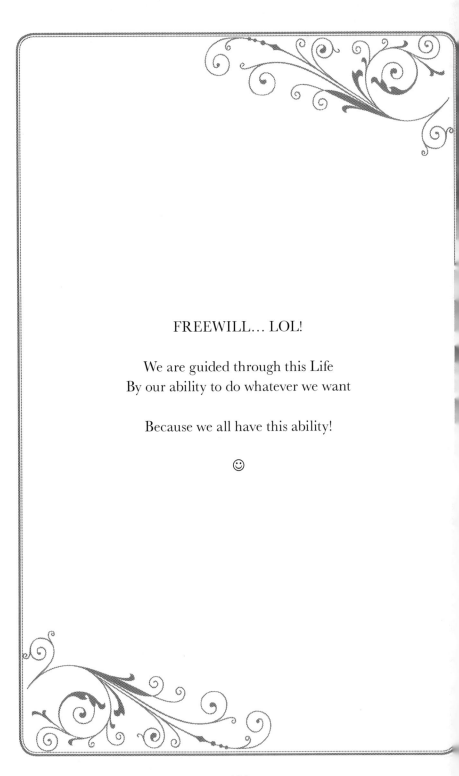

FREEWILL... LOL!

We are guided through this Life
By our ability to do whatever we want

Because we all have this ability!

☺

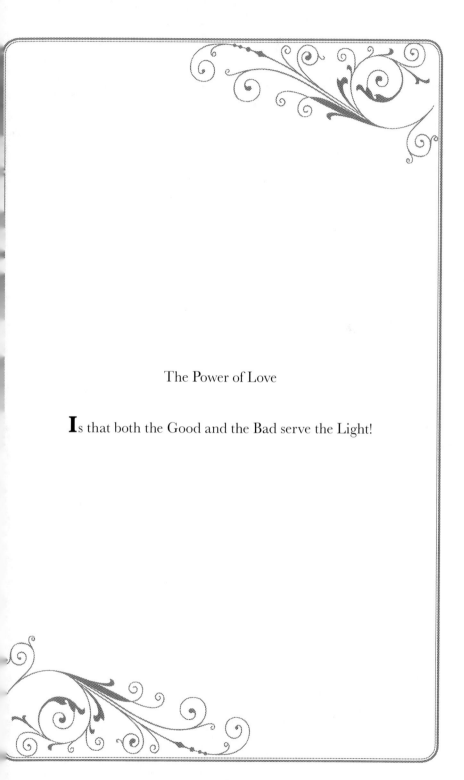

The Power of Love

Is that both the Good and the Bad serve the Light!

Have Fun!

Love a person in their happiness
And you teach them
To accept their own happiness
But try and Love an unhappy person
And you reject your own Happiness!

How can you not see
That your broken Heart created me
And was in your chest
Far before I came to be
A reflection of the pain
That in yourself you could not see
That only revealed
A broken Heart
I could not see
That hide in me?

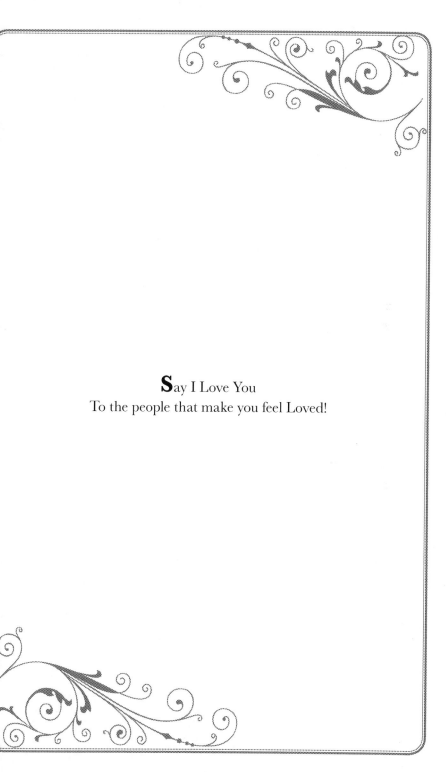

Say I Love You
To the people that make you feel Loved!

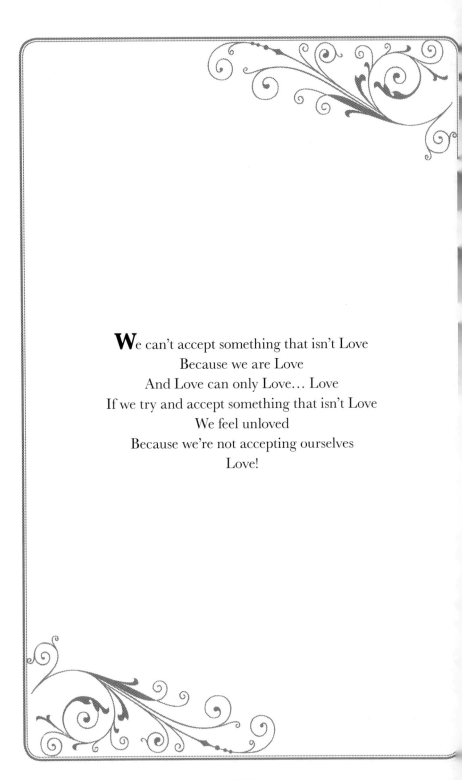

We can't accept something that isn't Love
Because we are Love
And Love can only Love... Love
If we try and accept something that isn't Love
We feel unloved
Because we're not accepting ourselves
Love!

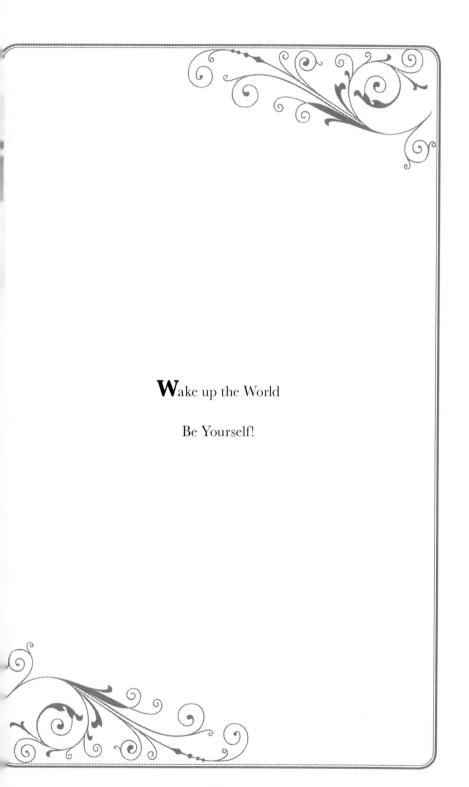

Wake up the World

Be Yourself!

Think Love
Feel Love
Live in Love
But don't accept a Life
Or a person
That refuses to give you Love
Because in doing so
You Deny Love
In doing so
You deny yourself
And you are Love
If you vibrate Love
So be Love
Be yourself!

The beauty of Love
Will be invisible to those that can't see themselves
But it will be seen and felt in the Heart
Of the person that chooses to Love them self!

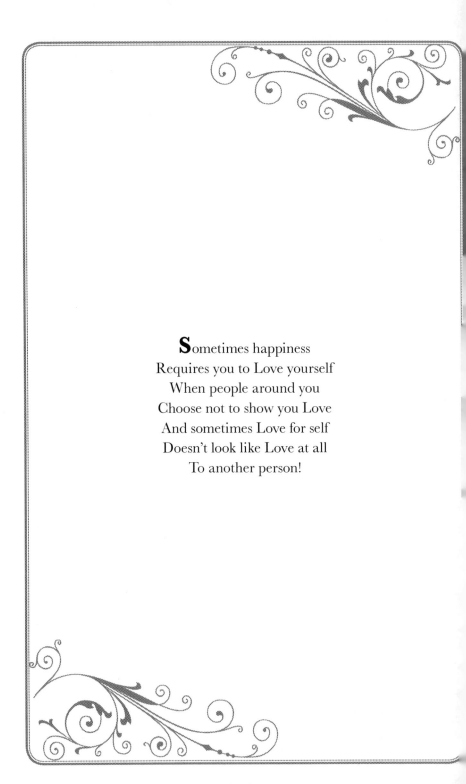

Sometimes happiness
Requires you to Love yourself
When people around you
Choose not to show you Love
And sometimes Love for self
Doesn't look like Love at all
To another person!

I Love You
Even if I choose not to show you Love
Because I show you where you choose not to give yourself love!

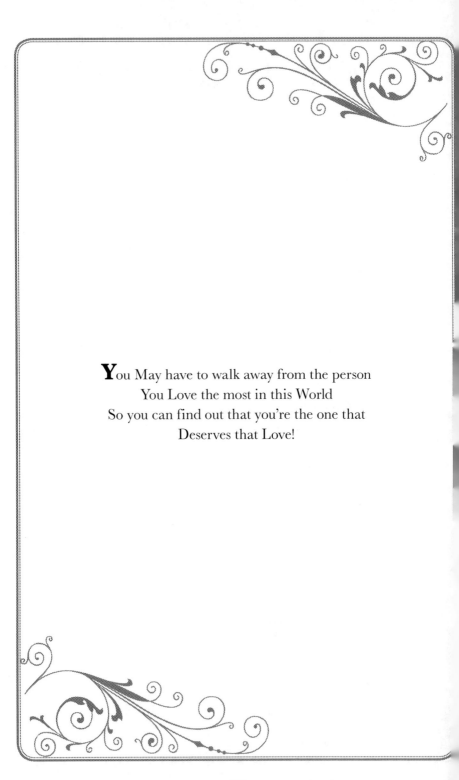

You May have to walk away from the person
You Love the most in this World
So you can find out that you're the one that
Deserves that Love!

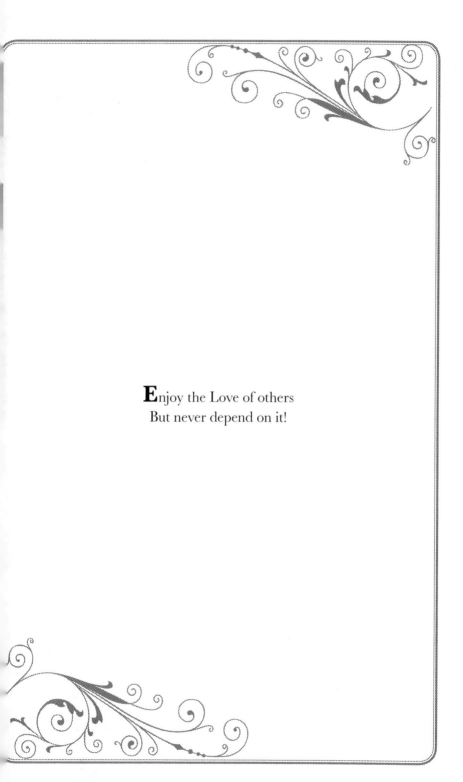

Enjoy the Love of others
But never depend on it!

QUESTION...

Why does Love confuse so many people?
And why does it seem to disappoint the ones who believe
In it the most?

ANSWER...
Because unexpressed negative emotion
Is the energy that fills your body!

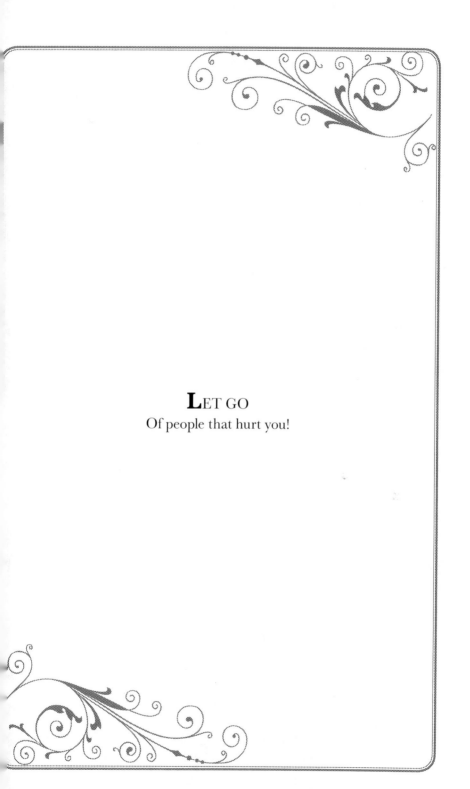

LET GO
Of people that hurt you!

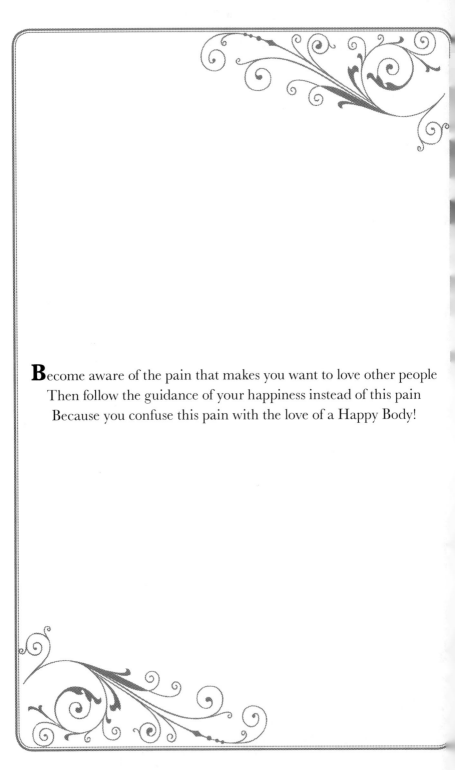

Become aware of the pain that makes you want to love other people
Then follow the guidance of your happiness instead of this pain
Because you confuse this pain with the love of a Happy Body!

Does it feel good to you?

If it doesn't then don't accept it!

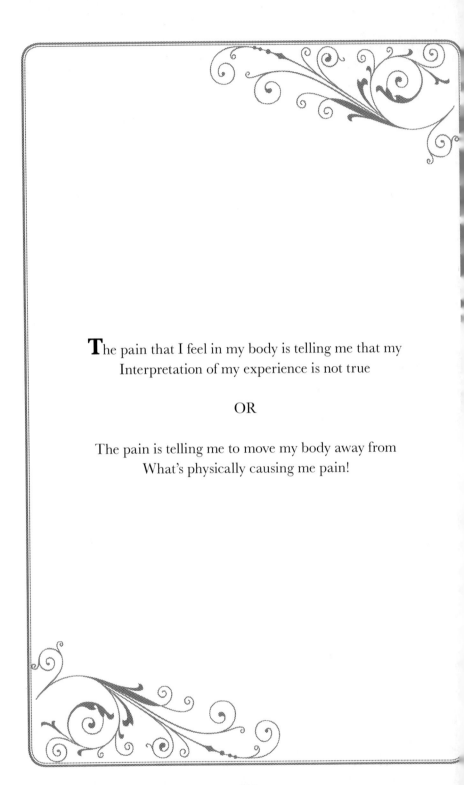

The pain that I feel in my body is telling me that my
Interpretation of my experience is not true

OR

The pain is telling me to move my body away from
What's physically causing me pain!

A Mind and Body that don't receive Love

Can't function in Love!

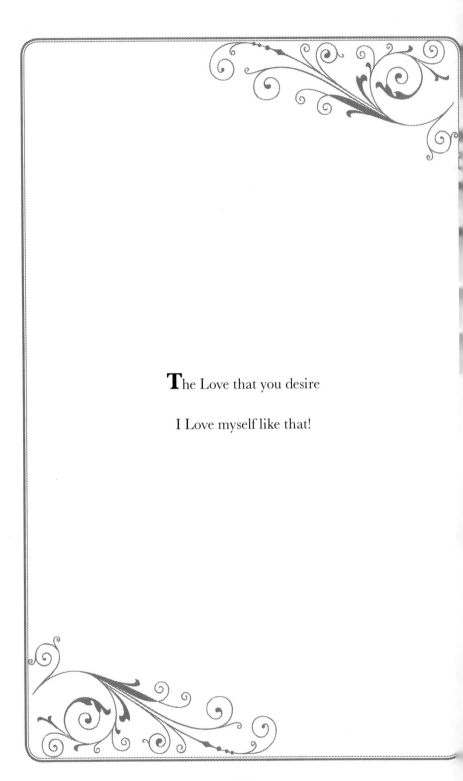

The Love that you desire

I Love myself like that!

Remove the Belief

That separates you from yourself
And be authentic in expressing who you are!

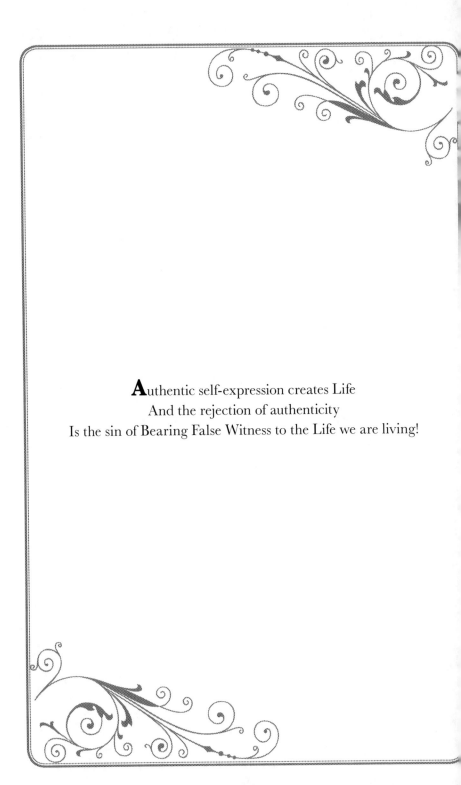

Authentic self-expression creates Life
And the rejection of authenticity
Is the sin of Bearing False Witness to the Life we are living!

AM I?

If I accept myself

I AM!

If I don't...

Then I am somebody else!

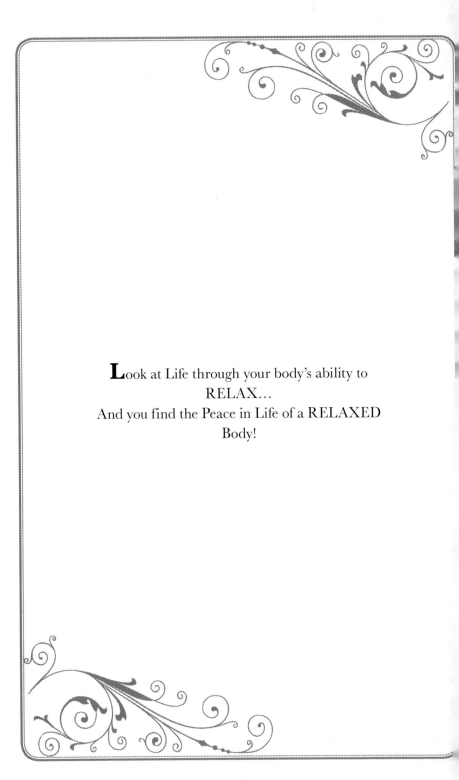

Look at Life through your body's ability to
RELAX...
And you find the Peace in Life of a RELAXED
Body!

Both Fear and Love are true expressions of Human Life
But both end the same way they start!

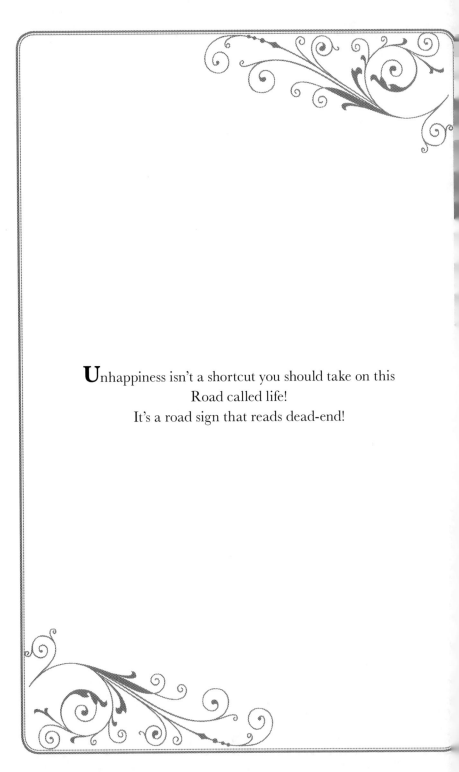

Unhappiness isn't a shortcut you should take on this
Road called life!
It's a road sign that reads dead-end!

Just keep choosing SELF LOVE
To the best of your ability!

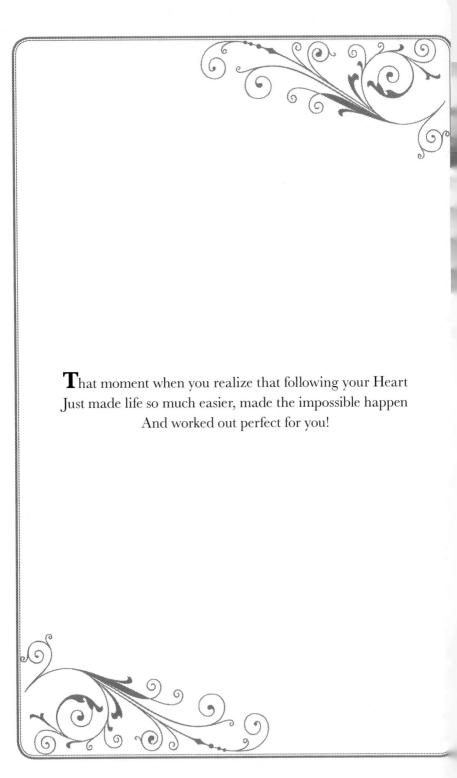

That moment when you realize that following your Heart
Just made life so much easier, made the impossible happen
And worked out perfect for you!

And then you realized
The Power of following
What opens the Heart
You found your Health
You Found your Happiness
And you Remembered!

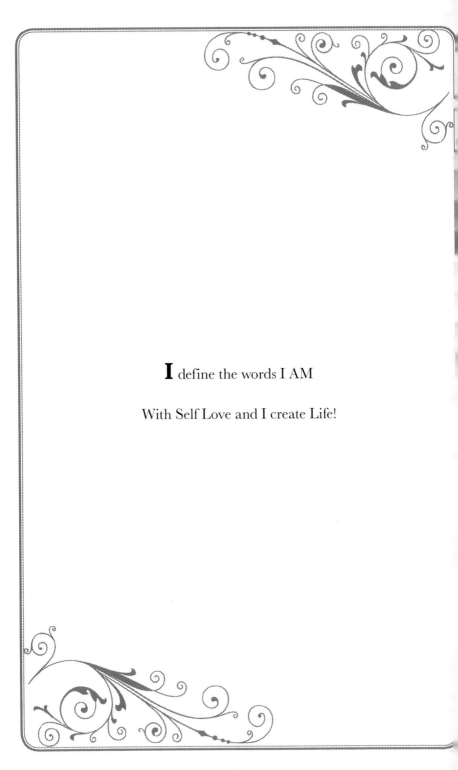

I define the words I AM

With Self Love and I create Life!

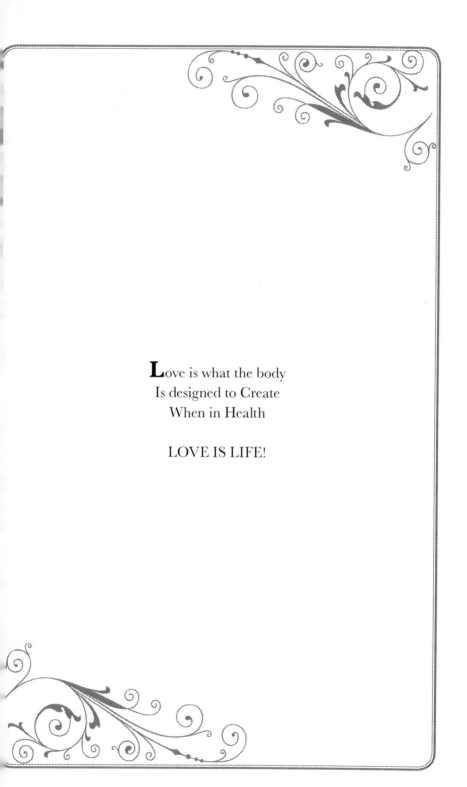

Love is what the body
Is designed to Create
When in Health

LOVE IS LIFE!

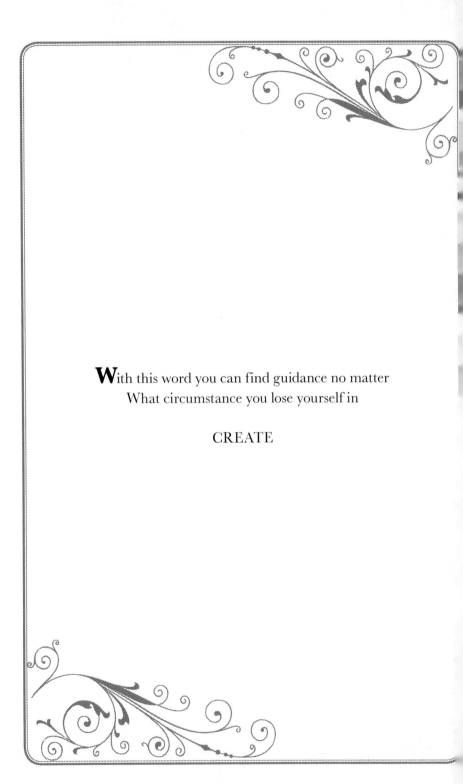

With this word you can find guidance no matter
What circumstance you lose yourself in

CREATE

Maybe you need to find the feeling you get from a
Creative Expression
Then as you Creations come to Life
You find happiness in being yourself through your
Creative Expression
And no longer need struggle to remind you of the
Happiness
You are here in this World to Create!

Create thought that inspires you!

CREATE KNOWLEDGE
That will bridge the gap between where we're at right now
And the full acceptance
Of the Health and Happiness of Self Love!

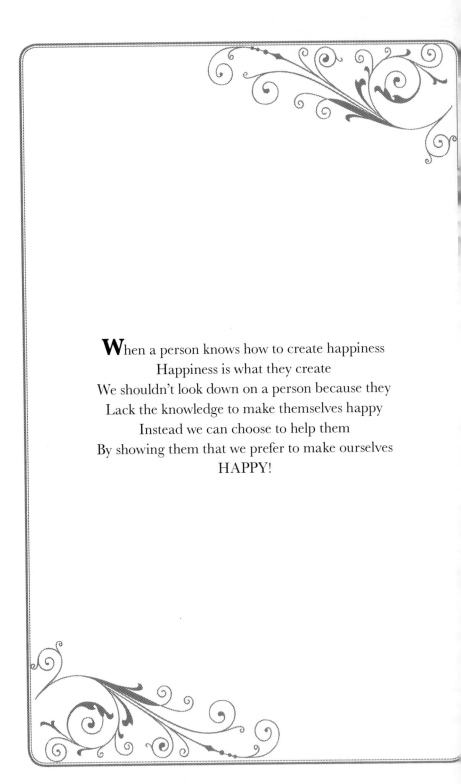

When a person knows how to create happiness
Happiness is what they create
We shouldn't look down on a person because they
Lack the knowledge to make themselves happy
Instead we can choose to help them
By showing them that we prefer to make ourselves
HAPPY!

Find a creative way to make a stranger Smile
The Smile on their face puts Happiness
In both of your Hearts!

On the go affirmation

I am a Laugh I am a Giggle
I am a Smile!

☺

I Love Smiles
I said this out loud as I typed this and my two year
Old son whispers to me…

ME TO!

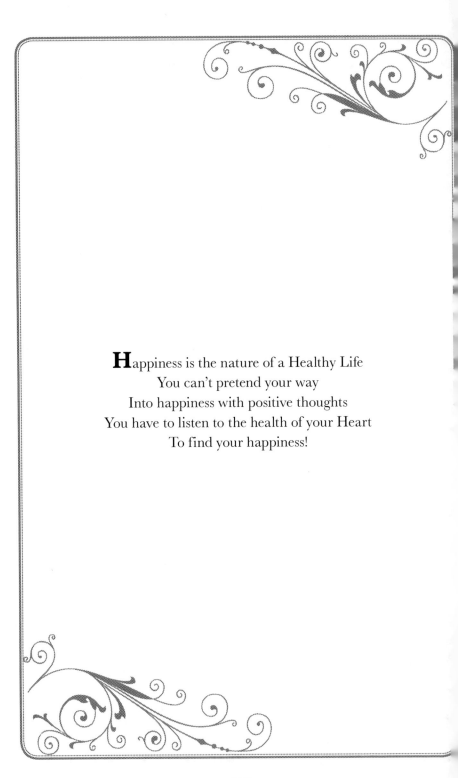

Happiness is the nature of a Healthy Life
You can't pretend your way
Into happiness with positive thoughts
You have to listen to the health of your Heart
To find your happiness!

You don't have to accept anything in Life
That makes you unhappy
But if you accepted a Life that makes you unhappy
It might be a little difficult to get away from it

☺

QUESTIONS TO ASK YOURSELF

How are my relationships teaching me self-love?
How is my diet teaching me self-love?
How are my thoughts teaching me self-love?
How do my emotions teach me self-love?
What can I learn about self-love in the environment I'm in?
How is my career teaching me self-love?
In what ways would Life have me accept myself today?

ASK YOURSELF

Do I have a guard on my Heart?
Am I trying to protect myself?
Or
Am I following my happiness?

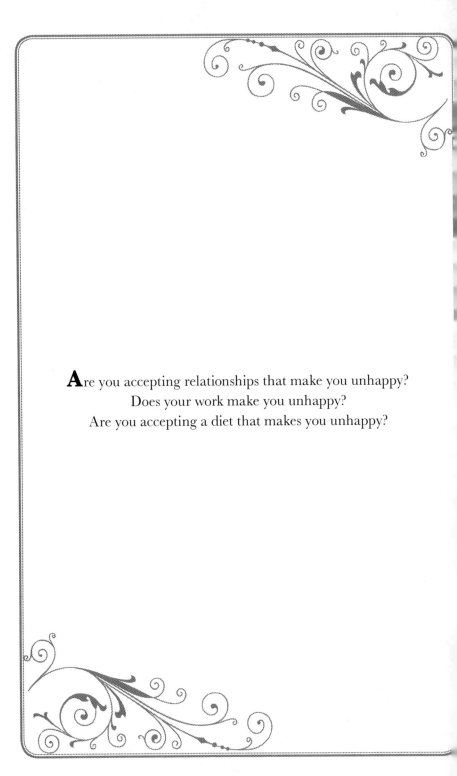

Are you accepting relationships that make you unhappy?
Does your work make you unhappy?
Are you accepting a diet that makes you unhappy?

Do you know what makes you happy?
Do you know what makes you… you?

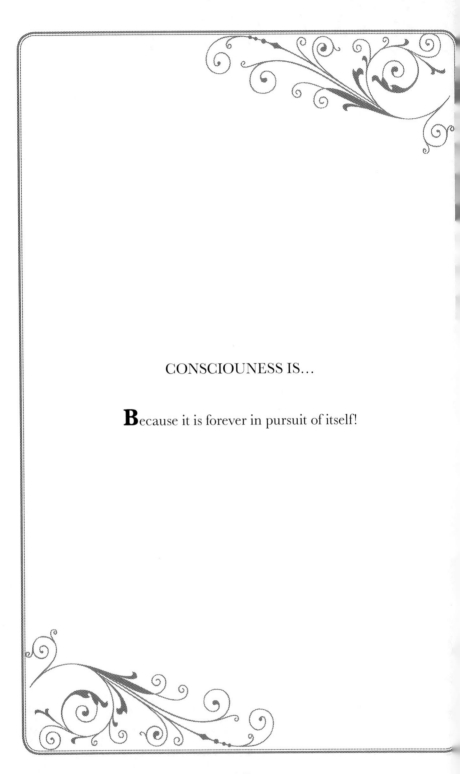

CONSCIOUNESS IS…

Because it is forever in pursuit of itself!

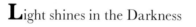

Light shines in the Darkness

So we walk into the Darkness to shine our Light!

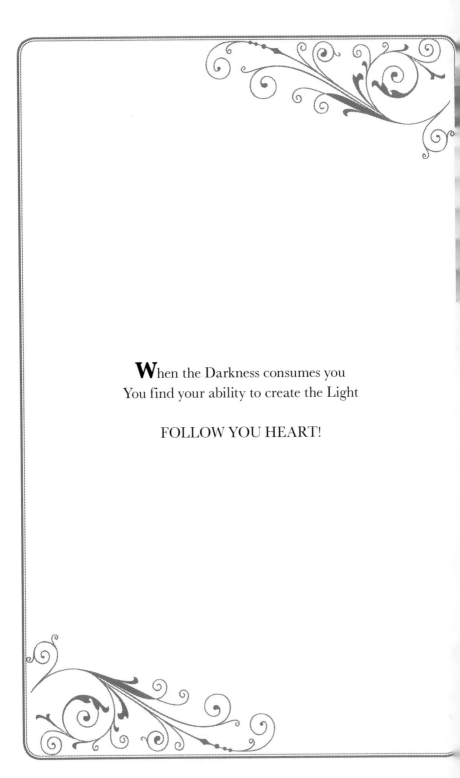

When the Darkness consumes you
You find your ability to create the Light

FOLLOW YOU HEART!

I Create Life
I forget about it
Then I Remember
This... I AM
The Life
Of my Creation
Then I do this
Over and over again
As I Create the Light
Of who I AM

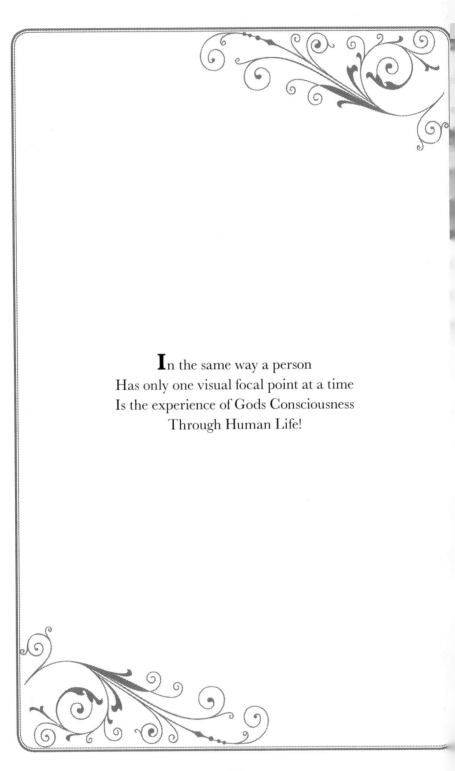

In the same way a person
Has only one visual focal point at a time
Is the experience of Gods Consciousness
Through Human Life!

TRY TO SOLVE THIS GOD PROBLEM

As God comes into physical form
From Oneness
This Oneness that God is
Then has to learn to embrace its Oneness
In many forms all at the same time
Without rejecting the expression of Oneness
In any form
While listening to the desire for Oneness
As it learns the expression of Oneness
In the form that it lives in

GET IT...?

☺

LIFE... LOL!

In a World where Religious and spiritual beliefs
Have taught us to reject ourselves
Because we are sinners
Or because we have an Ego
And Education has made us feel like
We have to reject ourselves
To follow the ideas of professionals
And businesses teach us to reject ourselves
For the good of the business
And parents teach us to reject ourselves
With discipline or a lack of it
WHAT WE REALLY NEED IN THIS WORLD
IS A MOVEMENT OF SELF-ACCEPTANCE
And an understanding of how self-acceptance is the
Same thing as the acceptance of Life…
The Earth the Sky the Water and the Light
And an understanding of how this can create
Health and Happiness

For ALL PEOPLE

We are resurrected when we come back to
The acceptance of the things that create life
Because then we find the Health
And Happiness of Life

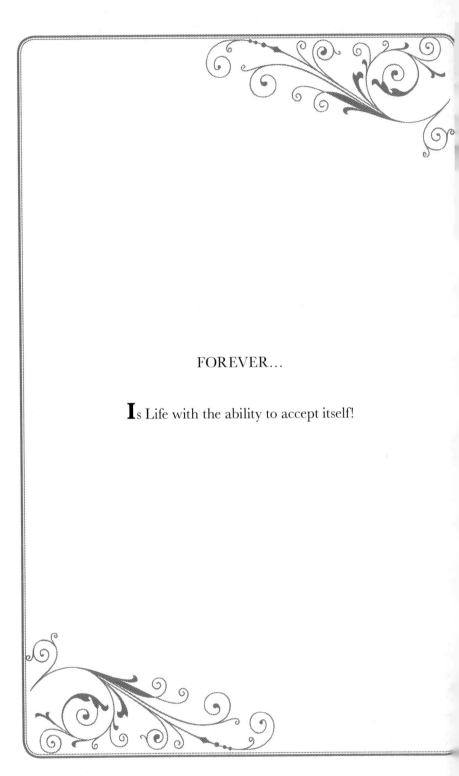

FOREVER…

Is Life with the ability to accept itself!

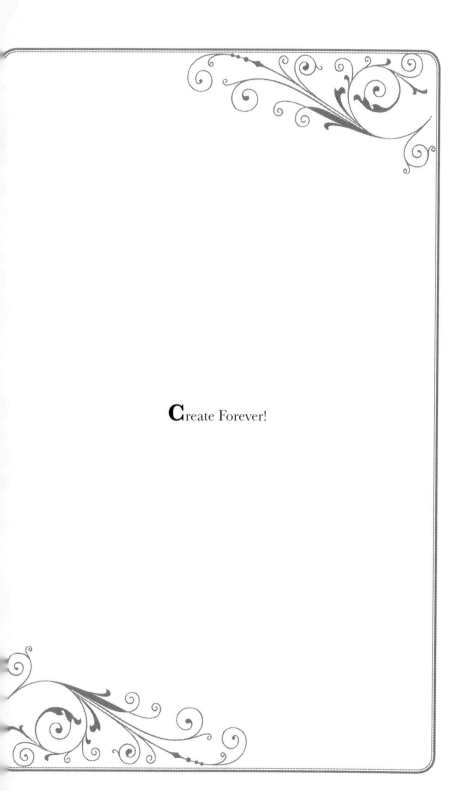

Create Forever!

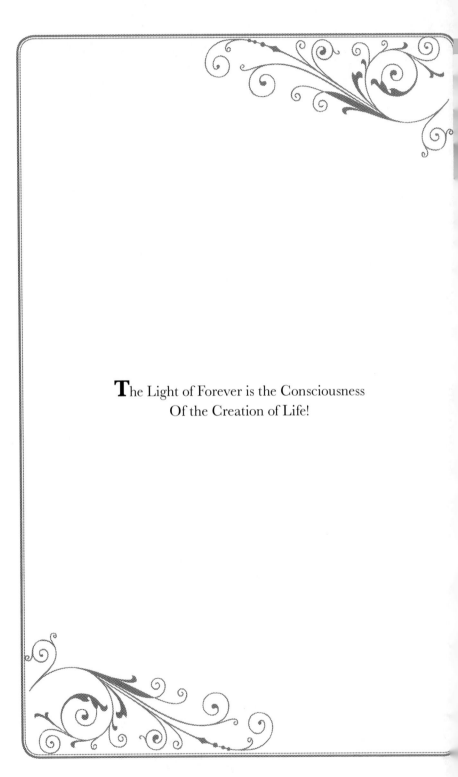

The Light of Forever is the Consciousness
Of the Creation of Life!

In the way that Life
Grows to Death
All Knowledge Grows
To its own End
But in the End
Is yet another beginning
A new way for Life
To learn SELF LOVE!

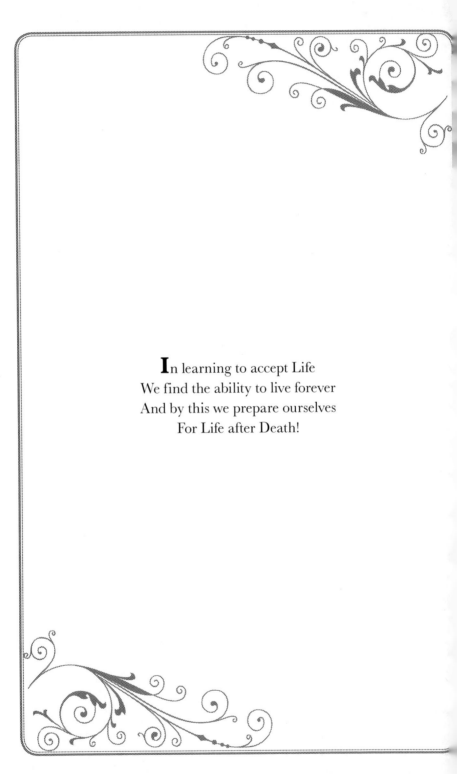

In learning to accept Life
We find the ability to live forever
And by this we prepare ourselves
For Life after Death!

The beat of your Heart
Vibrates the energy of who you are
Out of the body and into the Life around you
And this Energy is the Consciousness
Of your life after death!

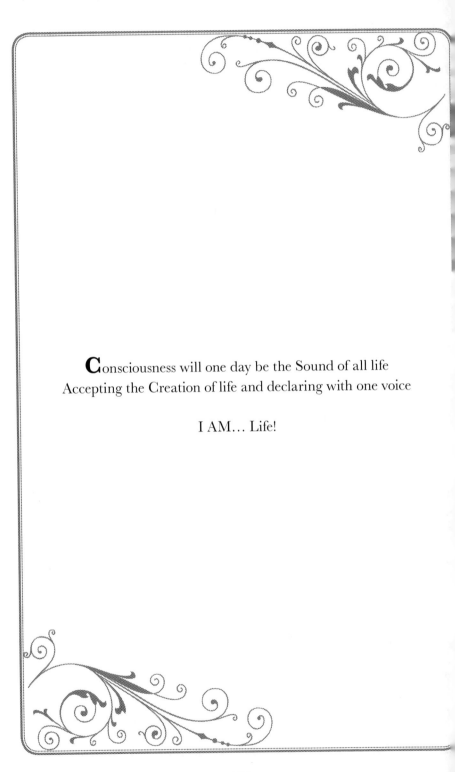

Consciousness will one day be the Sound of all life
Accepting the Creation of life and declaring with one voice

I AM... Life!

We will grow
The Knowledge of the acceptance of Life
To its greatest potential!
And in doing this
End the cycle of Life and Death!

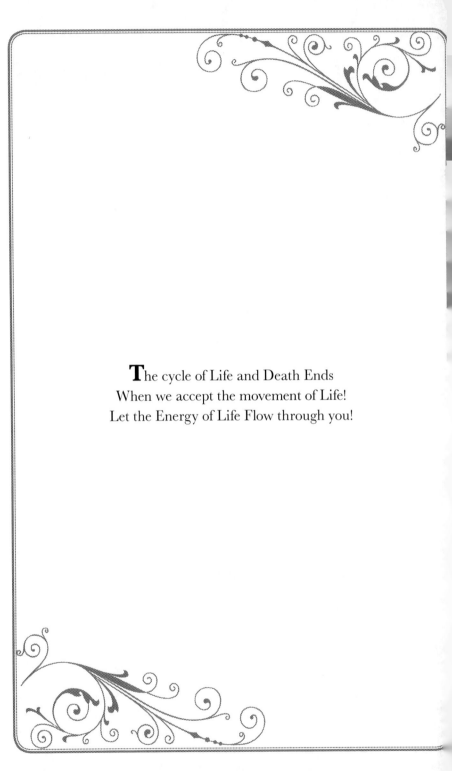

The cycle of Life and Death Ends
When we accept the movement of Life!
Let the Energy of Life Flow through you!

QUESTION… How do I live forever?

ANSWER…
All that you really need to do
Is Love the Body you live in
Love the natural World (what creates the body)
Love what you do!
And CREATE more of what you Love!

LOL… ☺

LET LIFE LIVE!

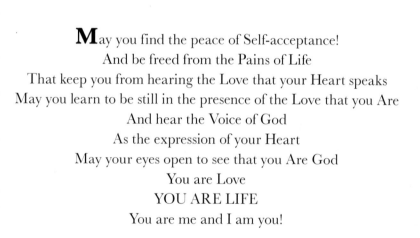

May you find the peace of Self-acceptance!
And be freed from the Pains of Life
That keep you from hearing the Love that your Heart speaks
May you learn to be still in the presence of the Love that you Are
And hear the Voice of God
As the expression of your Heart
May your eyes open to see that you Are God
You are Love
YOU ARE LIFE
You are me and I am you!

I AM GOD… And so are you!
And we came here to Create Life
To Create… LIGHT

Why did God laugh?

Because he told us to Be Still
So we could figure out
That Life itself is movement!

☺

Printed in the United States
By Bookmasters